Internet of Things Using Single Board Computers

Principles of IoT and Python Programming

G. R. Kanagachidambaresan

Apress®

Internet of Things Using Single Board Computers: Principles of IoT and Python Programming

G. R. Kanagachidambaresan
Chennai, India

ISBN-13 (pbk): 978-1-4842-8107-9   ISBN-13 (electronic): 978-1-4842-8108-6
https://doi.org/10.1007/978-1-4842-8108-6

Managing Director, Apress Media LLC: Welmoed Spahr
Acquisitions Editor: Aaron Black
Development Editor: James Markham
Coordinating Editor: Jessica Vakili
Copyeditor: Kim Burton

Distributed to the book trade worldwide by Springer Science+Business Media New York, 233 Spring Street, 6th Floor, New York, NY 10013. Phone 1-800-SPRINGER, fax (201) 348-4505, e-mail orders-ny@springer-sbm.com, or visit www.springeronline.com. Apress Media, LLC is a California LLC and the sole member (owner) is Springer Science + Business Media Finance Inc (SSBM Finance Inc). SSBM Finance Inc is a **Delaware** corporation.

For information on translations, please e-mail booktranslations@springernature.com; for reprint, paperback, or audio rights, please e-mail bookpermissions@springernature.com.

Apress titles may be purchased in bulk for academic, corporate, or promotional use. eBook versions and licenses are also available for most titles. For more information, reference our Print and eBook Bulk Sales web page at http://www.apress.com/bulk-sales.

Any source code or other supplementary material referenced by the author in this book is available to readers on the Github repository: https://github.com/Apress/Internet-of-Things-Using-Single-Board-Computers. For more detailed information, please visit http://www.apress.com/source-code.

Printed on acid-free paper

To my family, students, dear friends, and scholars

I specially dedicate this to my son, Ananthajith K

Table of Contents

About the Author

G. R. Kanagachidambaresan completed his PhD in Information and Communication Engineering from Anna University, Chennai, in 2017. He is currently an associate professor in the CSE Department at Vel Tech Rangarajan Dr. Sagunthala R&D Institute of Science and Technology. He is also a visiting professor at the University of Johannesburg.

His main research interest includes the Internet of Things, Industry 4.0, body sensor network, and fault-tolerant wireless sensor network. He has published several reputed articles and undertaken several consultancy activities for leading MNC companies. He has guest-edited several special issue volumes and books and served as an editorial review board member for peer-reviewed journals. He is TEC committee member in DBT, GOI, India.

He is presently working on several government-sponsored research projects like ISRO, DBT, and DST. He is Wiley's editor-in-chief of the Next Generation Computer and Communication Engineering Series. He is also the managing director for Eazythings Technology Private Limited.

About the Technical Reviewer

 **Massimo Nardone** has more than 22 years of experience in security, web/mobile development, cloud, and IT architecture. His true IT passions are security and Android.

He has been programming and teaching how to program with Android, Perl, PHP, Java, VB, Python, C/C++, and MySQL for more than 20 years.

He has a master of science degree in computing science from the University of Salerno, Italy.

He has worked as a project manager, software engineer, research engineer, chief security architect, information security manager, PCI/SCADA auditor, and senior lead IT security/cloud/SCADA architect for many years.

Acknowledgments

My heartfelt thanks to Apress, especially Jessica Vakili and Susan McDermott, for helping me throughout this project.

I sincerely thank the Department of BioTechnology (DBT-India) for their funding (BT/PR38273/AAQ/3/980/2020) on the smart aquaculture project.

I would also like to extend thanks to my JRFs: Ms. Meenakshi KV, Mr. M. Akash, Ms. A. V. Anandhalekshmi, and Ms. V. Sowmiya.

I give special thanks to my son Mr. Ananthajith K, my wife, Dr. Mahima V, my parents, Mr. G. S. Ramasubramanian and Mrs. Lalitha, and Mrs. Chandra, Mr. Venkatraman, Mrs. V. Chitra, and Mr. V. Bharath for their timely support.

Preface

The rapid growth of technology and new smart, sustainable development initiatives has made the Internet of Things (IoT) and edge analytics an inevitable platform for all engineering domains. The need for a sophisticated and ambient environment has resulted in an exponential growth in automation and artificial intelligence. The right sensor or actuator, a specific processor, and the correct transmission unit can offer the best solution to any IoT problem. Lightweight machine learning or mathematical logic can bring a good solution to existing smart-city problems.

This book provides detailed information on sensors, their interfacing connections, programming with single-board computers, and creating integrated projects with a combination of sensors, processors, and actuators. A detailed introduction to Python and Arduino-based programming is also discussed to kindle interest in IoT programming. IoT products' wired and wireless connections are discussed, and programming examples are provided.

This is a completely new textbook that reflects recent developments while providing a comprehensive introduction to the fields of IoT, single-board computers, and Python programming. It is aimed at advanced undergraduates as well as researchers and practitioners. This book deals more with electronics and programming than simple text. It best suits outcome-based education systems and can aid industry-ready IoT engineers.

Funding Information

The part of this book is supported by the Department of Biotechnology funding information (BT/PR38273/AAQ/3/980/2020).

CHAPTER 1

An Overview of the Internet of Things (IoT) and Sensors

Recent advancements in single-board computers (SBCs) [16] and boards have made the Internet of Things (IoT) more accessible and easier to use. The complete automation, information analysis from sensor data, and integration of individual components with IoT systems helps to build new Smart environment solutions. The scope of the areas is broadened with IoT components and sensors.

IoT uses existing and emerging technology for event detection and automation. IoT has the advantages of recent software advancements, reducing hardware prices and available technology options. It created a great change in product delivery and services and a major revolution in Industry 4.0. Figure 1-1 illustrates the key features of IoT.

© G. R. Kanagachidambaresan 2022
G. R. Kanagachidambaresan, *Internet of Things Using Single Board Computers*,
https://doi.org/10.1007/978-1-4842-8108-6_1

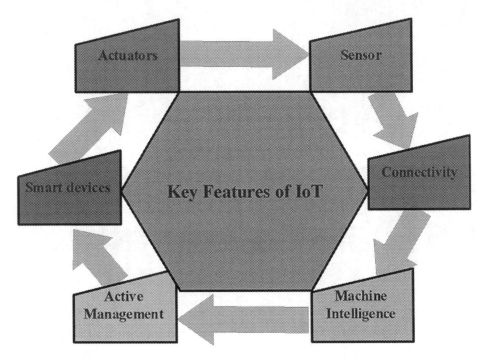

Figure 1-1. *IoT feature and data flow*

Sensors

Sensors are the main data acquisition and detection system, which converts any physical quantity (i.e., event) into a signal. In some sensors, direct conversion takes place; in others, multiple conversions take place to attain accuracy and quantification. Some of the sensors used in IoT and prototyping are shown in Figure 1-2. Sensors are collectively connected with an A/D converter to convert their signals to digital forms so that a processor understands and can program effectively. Figure 1-2 illustrates sensor classification (mode of operation, signal output, and energy-based).

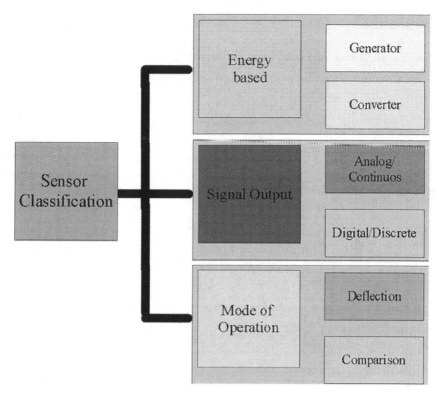

Figure 1-2. *Sensor type classification*

Next, let's further discuss sensor type classification.

Energy-based
Generator

Energy generation–based sensors provides conversion energy conversion, like voltage and current, on any physical event. For example, a piezoelectric sensor converts vibration energy to a proportional voltage. The seebeck metal junction converts the change in temperature to proportional energy conversion.

Conversion

Sensors convert one mode of physical quantity to another; for example, an anemometer converts air velocity to rotational motion, which is further converted to electrical voltage for measurement. These sensors are operated in a proportional zone for calibration and stable operation. Most sensors provide linear data conversion.

Signal Output

Analog

Sensors such as anemometers provide analog conversion of data. Analog signal from annemometer is converted to digital data with the help of an analog-to-digital converter. The sensor's frequency of operation should be far greater than the frequency of the physical quantity to get clear information after digital conversion.

Discrete

Cameras and tile-based sensors provide discrete and digital information directly to the processor. This makes the sensor easy to integrate with any digital processor.

Mode of Operation

Sensors are deflection- or comparison-based. Deflection happens when sensing a physical event. This is normally an angular-based movement between two points. Comparison-based meters normally work with standard available data. GPS sensors provide comparison-based sensing.

- Deflection (e.g., voltage meters and current meters)

- Comparison (e.g., GPS sensors)

Electronic Sensors

Figure 1-3 illustrates sensor classification based on the field of operation, such as mechanical, optical, electrical, acoustic, thermal, chemical, radiation, biological, and magnetic.

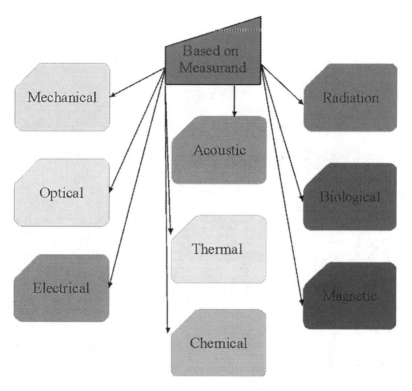

Figure 1-3. *Sensor classification based on measurand*

Mechanical

- Linear and angular position
- Velocity of the subject
- Acceleration

- Force

- Viscosity, rigidness, and roughness

- Pressure and stress

- Strain

- Mass and density measurement

Optical

- Wave velocity

- Polarization and spectrum

- Wave amplitude

Electrical

- Conductivity

- Potential difference

- Charge and current density

- Field

Thermal

- Heat flux

- Thermal conductivity

Chemical

- States and identifies

- Color change

- Change in voltage

Radiation

- Energy

- Intensity

Biological

- Mass

- Concentration

- States

- Magnetic

- Magnetic field

- Magnetic flux

- Permeability

Connectivity

Figure 1-4 illustrates the connectivity features of IoT communication.

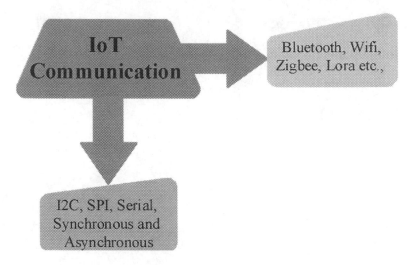

Figure 1-4. *IoT connectivity features*

Bluetooth Low Energy, Zigbee, LoRa, and Wi-Fi are the most common types of connectivity in an IoT environment. I2C, SPI, and Rx-Tx serial communication protocols are examples of wired connectivity.

Bluetooth

Bluetooth network technology creates a personal area network (PAN) by wirelessly connecting mobile devices over a short distance. The Bluetooth architecture has its own independent model with a stack of protocols; it does not follow the standard OSI or TCP/IP models.

Zigbee

The Zigbee 3.0 protocol [1] is an IEEE 802.15.4 specification that supports a 2.4 GHz frequency band. The following are some of the features of Zigbee 3.0.

- Low power: Devices that comply with Zigbee 3.0 consume less power and transmit data at a slower rate. For IoT devices, long-lasting batteries are required. As a result, the Internet of Things (IoT) network extensively uses this standard.

- Reliable and robust: The mesh topology of the Zigbee 3.0 network eliminates single points of failure and ensures packet delivery reliability.

- Scalable: Devices can be added to a Zigbee 3.0 network anytime.

- It is a secure network because it employs AES-128 encryption.

- Global standard: Zigbee 3.0 devices use the 2.4 GHz frequency band, which is widely used worldwide. As a result, it has become the industry standard around the world.

Wi-Fi

Wi-Fi [2] is a technology that transfers data through radio waves that can make small gadgets exchange data connected within a small router. Wi-Fi uses the Institute of Electrical and Electronics Engineers' (IEEE) 802.11 standards for effective data transmission.

IEEE 802.11 devices have the primary benefit of making it easier to deploy local area networks (LANs) at a lower cost. They can host wireless LANs in outdoor areas and airports, where running cables to every device isn't practical.

LoRa

LoRa [3] is a long-range wireless communication technology derived from the CSS chirp-based spread spectrum. The chirp pulses communicate information, similar to BATS communication.

Wired Communication

I²C

I²C (Inter-Integrated Circuit) [4] is a two-wired communication protocol (see Figure 1-5). It is a bus interface, serial communication protocol built into devices. It has recently become a popular protocol for short-distance communication.

Only two bidirectional open-drain lines—SDA (Serial Data) and SCL (Serial Clock)—are used for data communication. Both lines are cranked up. The SDA pin sends and receives data. SCL carries the clock signal.

I2C has two modes of operation: master and slave. Master mode is the most advanced mode.

Slave mode obeys the command from the master and transmits or receives data accordingly.

Each clock's high to low pulse on the SCL line synchronizes each data bit transferred on the SDA line. Figure 1-5 shows I²C communication protocols.

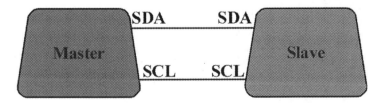

Figure 1-5. *I²C communication protocols*

SPI

The data communication module uses SDA and SCL dual connection lines. SDA receives and transmits data. Serial Peripheral Interface (SPI) communication is mainly used by components such as RTC, A-to-D converters, and other computer peripherals. SPI [5] communication uses a full duplex synchronous communication protocol that works in serial mode between the master and slave devices. Figure 1-6 illustrates SPI communication protocols.

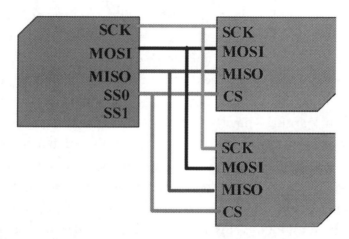

Figure 1-6. *SPI communication protocols*

Serial Communication

Serial communication is a straightforward and dependable way to send data over long distances. RS-232 is a widely used serial communication protocol. The data in this standard is sent in serial format at a preset speed (called a *baud rate/number*) of bits communicated between the sender and receiver. Common baud rates are 4800, 9600, 19200, and 38400. Figure 1-7 shows the connection diagram for the UART communication scheme.

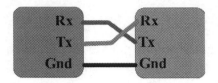

Figure 1-7. *UART data communication*

Machine Intelligence

Machine intelligence [14] attempts to program a computer to perform previously human-only tasks. In general, the learning process in intelligent machines entails gathering information about their environment, deploying that information to build knowledge about it, and then generalizing that knowledge base to deal with environmental uncertainty.

Two machine intelligence techniques—imitation learning and reinforcement learning—have been developed to help machines learn. The learning algorithms are opted based on consideration of tasks and their characteristics. Intelligent systems are an option to collect data from the agents and acquire knowledge about its surrounding, and the computation is adapted for the environment. To maintain control over a society of autonomous agents, the agents' learning process requires a self-organizing mechanism. It should be noted that imbuing intelligent machines with the capacity to learn is a difficult task; however, the capacity to learn is what defines a machine as intelligent. Figure 1-8 illustrates machine learning classification based on input data.

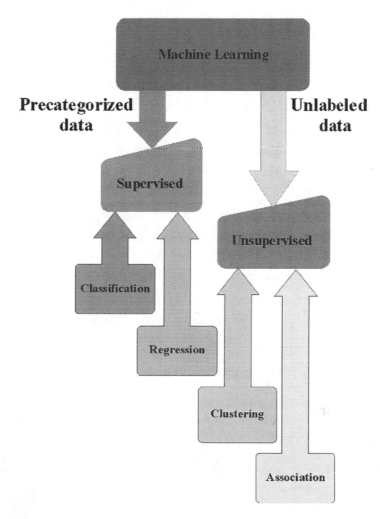

Figure 1-8. *Classical machine learning domains*

The supervised learning module predicts category (classification module) and number (regression module). Unsupervised learning provides clustering, dimension reduction, and association modules.

Active Management

The main components and operation of a closed-loop sensor management system are depicted in Figure 1-9. The raw sensor data is processed for information relevant to the sensing objective when the sensor is chosen, and a measurement is taken. This usually requires the fusion of data from several sensing modalities (e.g., optical and acoustic) and other properties, as well as the addition of information from earlier measurements and possibly other sources. Auxiliary information, such as target tracks or choices about non-sensor manager-related concerns, may be generated by the loop's fusion and signal processing. For sensor management reasons, they must generate a state of information that allows quantification of the benefits of each feasible sensor selection in the following time epoch. Currently, accessible quantification methodologies range from statistical (e.g., mean risk or knowledge gain) to entirely heuristic. The sensor management must then optimize which sensor to use for the next measurement.

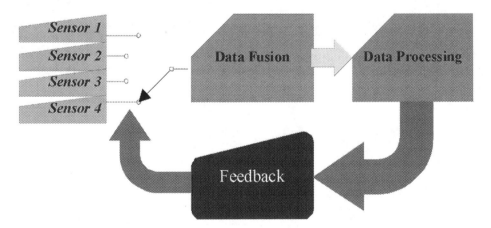

Figure 1-9. *Data processing in IoT architecture*

The sensor selector provides information from a particular sensor module. Once data from a particular sensor is received, data fusion is done through a sensor data fusion algorithm. The signal is processed using algorithms. The data is corrected through closed-loop control system algorithms.

Sensor Fusion

Sensor fusion is a technique for reducing the amount of uncertainty in a robot's navigation or task performance by combining data from multiple sensors, as shown in Figure 1-10. Sensor fusion helps the robot create a more accurate world model, which allows it to navigate and behave better. There are three main methods for combining sensor data.

- Redundant sensors collect repeated information that is permanently fit in sources like heaters, gates, and other locations.

- Complementary sensors collect different information on events happening inside the monitoring environment.

- Coordinated sensors are logically operating sensor that collects information about the environment.

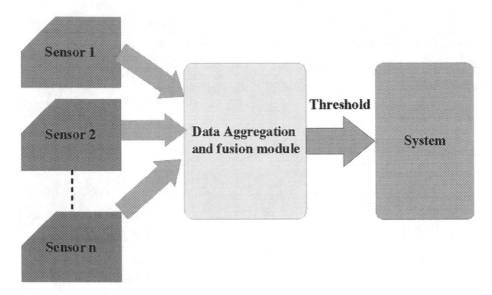

Figure 1-10. *Sensor data aggregation and fusion process*

To obtain high-quality, relevant measurement data, data fusion combines several sources of information utilizing mathematical methods and technical tools. Improved detectability and reliability, expanded range of spatial-temporal perception, reduced degree of inference ambiguity, improved detection accuracy, increased dimension of target features, improved resolution of spatial questions, and enhanced fault-tolerant fusion are all advantages of data fusion over independent processing of a single source.

Smart Devices

Human-Computer Interaction

Human-computer interaction (HCI) [6] is a subfield of computer science that investigates how people (users) interact with computers, as well as the design, evaluation, and implementation of user interfaces for computer systems that are responsive to the user's needs and habits. This multidisciplinary field incorporates computer science, behavioral sciences, and design. One of the primary goals of HCI is to make computer systems more accessible and useable. A user interface consists of hardware and software that allows users to modify the system while allowing the system to communicate with the user. HCI focuses on the design, implementation, and evaluation of user interfaces. In its broadest sense, HCI occurs when a human user and a computer system collaborate to achieve a goal. Usability is the part of human-computer interaction concerned with making it, among other things, successful, efficient, and enjoyable for the user. Usability entails usability, productivity, efficiency, effectiveness, learnability, retention, and user interest.

Context Awareness

Figure 1-11 depicts sensor data context awareness [7]. The sensor data and context awareness provide better infrastructure and ambiance.

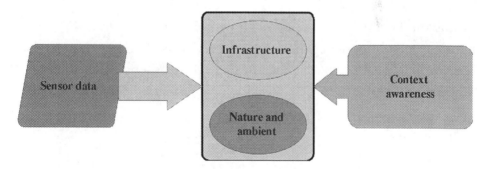

Figure 1-11. *Data awareness schemes in IoT*

Actuators

The applications in a smart city [10]—such as health care, smart agriculture, and other industrial applications—use actuators [8], such as drives, motors, and other physical signal converters. A *wireless sensor* and *actuator network* (WSAN) [9] comprises automated actuators. Microcomputers normally link directly to tiny actuators; however, heavy-load actuators are coupled via driver circuits. Linear and rotational moving actuators are the two types of actuators that move. A huge number of our daily demands, such as fans and escalators, are met by these actuators.

Electric, pneumatic, and hydraulic power sources are also used to classify them. Electric actuators are the most frequent, and PWM signals are generated by the system control actuators like servo and stepper motors. The significant change in the pulse width, time, and change in frequency is reflected in the actuator's velocity, rotational direction, and amount of torque exerted. Most actuators in the industry are actuated through PLC boards. This chapter showcases building prototypes with small servos and steppers, which are often accomplished using SBCs like Arduino and Raspberry Pi.

Table 1-1 describes the actuator types mentioned in this book, including micro steppers, SG90, and infrared. To keep things simple, these actuators are primarily programmed using Arduino and Raspberry Pi ideas.

Table 1-1. *Actuator Types*

S.No	Actuator type	Output	Operating range	Power required	Number of wire connection	External battery source required	Connectivity type Analog/i2c/spi, digital/ driver requirement
1	**Servo motor**	Angular motion	0-5 v	Less than 1W	3	Not necessary for low power	PWM
2	**Stepper motor**	Angular position	2.55 v-2.8 v	1.68 Amps	4	Yes	Drivers or DPDT relay
3	**Oled display**	Digital display	3.3V-5V 20mA max	3.3v	12C pins	yes	IIC & SPI

(continued)

Table 1-1. (*continued*)

S.No	Actuator type	Output	Operating range	Power required	Number of wire connection	External battery source required	Connectivity type Analog/i2c/spi, digital/ driver requirement
4	Relay	Mechanical contacts and solid state	5ms-20ms	5V	3	No (unless it's12V relay)	Both digital and analog
5	Solenoid	Mechanical energy angular motion	5-10ms 15-150ms	9-65W	2 terminals each	External regulator or separate power supply	Both digital and analog
6	IR led	Light	760-1nm Max = 780-50nm	1.2-3.4V	2 pins for each	no	Both digital and analog

7	**Heat exchanger**	Thermal	1000°C and 1000 bars	Not needed	Wires not needed	Acid batteries	Tube box
8	**Speaker**	Sound pressure level (SPL) in dB	60 Hz – 18 kHz	100 – 1000 watts	2 or more	No	Digital
9	**Linear actuator**	Straight line motion/ mechanical energy	5 lb – 10000 lb force	15 – 2000 pounds	4 pins	DC Battery	Digital

IoT and Smart City Applications

Automobile Sensors

Currently, modern automotive design can be accomplished using a variety of sensors [12]. These are integrated into the vehicle's engine to detect and resolve issues such as repairs and service. Sensors in automobiles keep an eye on the vehicle's operation. The owner of a car has no idea how many sensors their vehicle contains. Automobile sensors are sophisticated sensors that can monitor and control various parameters, including oil pressure, temperature, emission level, and coolant level. Numerous types of sensors are used in automobiles, but it is critical to understand how they work. To demonstrate the purpose of these sensors, the following is a list of the most frequently found sensors in automobiles. The sensor depicted in Figure 1-12 is used in automobile systems.

- Speed sensor for the engine

- Oxygen sensor for the exhaust manifold

- Mass airflow sensor for the exhaust manifold

- Fuel temperature sensor for the exhaust manifold

- Camshaft position sensor for the exhaust manifold

- Throttle position sensor for the exhaust manifold

- Vehicle speed sensor for the exhaust manifold

- Spark knock sensor for the exhaust manifold

- Coolant sensor for the exhaust manifold

- Voltage sensor for the exhaust manifold

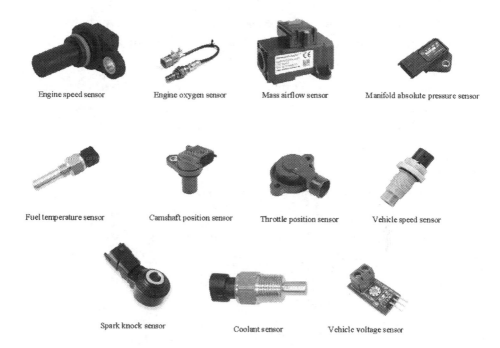

Engine speed sensor   Engine oxygen sensor   Mass airflow sensor   Manifold absolute pressure sensor

Fuel temperature sensor   Camshaft position sensor   Throttle position sensor   Vehicle speed sensor

Spark knock sensor   Coolant sensor   Vehicle voltage sensor

Figure 1-12. *Some important automobile sensors*

Smart Home Sensors

Smarter homes are established with IoT, cloud tech, and logical event processing. IoT allows mobile applications [11] with various sensors to be managed and communicated remotely. Sensors can monitor and regulate a variety of household appliances, such as air conditioning, lighting, and other environmental controls. As a result, it integrates computer intelligence with household equipment, allowing for temperature monitoring indoors and outdoors and appliance operation.

Cloud technology enables expandable processing energy, memory availability, apps for designing, administering, and operating home services, and remote control of home equipment. A rule-based event processing system manages an advanced smart home's overall control and orchestration. The term *smart home* refers to a domestic application of building automation that encompasses all embedded technology and its control and automation. It encompasses home appliances like air conditioning/heating systems, smart TVs, large appliances, and IP security cameras that can talk with their owner on a time and event basis through mobile phones and the Internet. The home electrical system is made of switches and sensors connected to a centralized IoT system operated by the homeowners and controlled via the cloud, GSM, and WLAN connectivity.

The main advantages include energy efficiency, security, reduced operating costs, and user sophistication. The convenience, cost, and reduced operating time provide plenty of energy savings to the users. These techs are more adaptable to changes in the needs of outpatients, such as post-surgical people recovering in their homes. Its architecture is frequently adaptable enough to integrate various devices from multiple manufacturers and standards. Figure 1-13 depicts the sensors used in a smart home system.

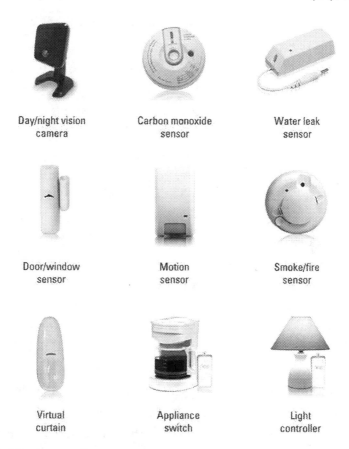

Figure 1-13. *Smart home sensors*

Smart Transportation Sensors

Improvements in ICT (Information and Communication Technology) devices have enabled opportunities for intelligent and sustainable transportation systems [13]. ICT in transportation helps sustainability, safety integration, and high-speed, accurate responses. The primary expectation of people using intelligent transportation like fast mobility, environmental sustainability, and economic development through goods and service transportation can be done through ICT tools. The platform used by *intelligent transport systems* (ITS) to access, gather and assess precise environmental data is crucial to its operation.

There are typically two types of sensor platforms. The first is an intra-vehicle sensing platform that collects data about a vehicle's condition. The two approaches of sensing are used in ITS. An *intra-vehicle sensing platform* collects data about a vehicle's working conditions. An *urban sensing platform* gathers information about traffic conditions. Sensing technology has become essential for vehicle-to-vehicle (V2V) [15] and vehicle-to-infrastructure (V2I) communication. The data is further communicated to a *transportation management system* (TMS) for further data analysis and prognostics. The data can offer prognostics that can be used for decision-making, reducing pollution, emission traffic congestion, and road reconstruction.

Non-intrusive sensors offer information like the location of the signal acquired through GPS devices, traffic queue density through LIDAR and traffic conditions through combined GPS information, and road and weather conditions. Sensors, such as high traffic lights, are typically placed in higher positions to monitor the region of interest. These sensors are also mounted under bridges and directly beneath a surveillance zone. Some sensors are positioned at the ground level to detect pedestrians. These are mostly used for single lanes and unidirectional traffic due to their vulnerability to interference from neighboring objects. Figure 1-14 shows sensors utilized in intelligent transportation.

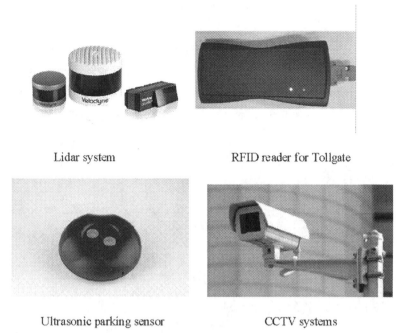

Lidar system   RFID reader for Tollgate

Ultrasonic parking sensor   CCTV systems

Figure 1-14. *List of sensors in transportation*

Non-invasive sensors can more effectively perform many intrusive sensor duties. Weather conditions, like rain, fog, snow, and dust pollution, significantly impact them. To make educated decisions about traffic improvement projects, precise traffic statistics are required. Drivers are more likely to detect non-intrusive sensors, leading to varied and faster responses, such as slowing down and driving in the proper lane. It is critical not only to install these sensors but also to reduce driver reaction times based on the collected data and provide a more realistic depiction of the context and reality of the road or avenue.

Summary

This chapter overviewed sensors, actuators, and other communication protocols. Various sensor usage with different applications was also addressed in this chapter. Sensor classification and interfacing with boards are discussed in the next chapter.

References

[1] S. Long and F. Miao, "Research on Zigbee wireless communication technology and its application," 2019 IEEE 4th Advanced Information Technology, Electronic and Automation Control Conference (IAEAC), pp. 1830–1834. doi: 10.1109/IAEAC47372.2019.8997928.

[2] K. Pahlavan and P. Krishnamurthy, "Evolution and Impact of Wi-Fi Technology and Applications: A Historical Perspective," *International Journal of Wireless Information Networks*, vol. 28, Nov. 19, 2020, pp. 3–19. https://doi.org/10.1007/s10776-020-00501-8.

[3] U. Noreen, A. Bounceur, and L. Clavier, "A study of LoRa low power and wide area network technology," 2017 International Conference on Advanced Technologies for Signal and Image Processing (ATSIP), pp. 1–6. doi: 10.1109/ATSIP.2017.8075570.

[4] Dawoud Shenouda Dawoud and Peter Dawoud, "Design of I2C Bus and Operation," in Microcontroller and Smart Home Networks, River Publishers, 2020, pp. 55–112.

[5] Dawoud Shenouda Dawoud, Peter Dawoud, "Serial Peripheral Interface (SPI)," in Serial Communication Protocols and Standards RS232/485, UART/USART, SPI, USB, INSTEON, Wi-Fi and WiMAX, River Publishers, 2020, pp.191–244.

[6] Erin T. Solovey and Felix Putze, Improving HCI with Brain Input: Review, Trends, and Outlook, Now Publishers, 2021.

[7] P. S. Gandodhar and S. M. Chaware, "Context Aware Computing Systems: A survey," 2018 2nd International Conference on I-SMAC (IoT in Social, Mobile, Analytics and Cloud), 2018, pp. 605–608.

[8] Jeffrey Wishart, Yan Chen, Steven Como, Narayanan Kidambi, Duo Lu, Yezhou Yang, "Sensor and Actuator Hardware," in Fundamentals of Connected and Automated Vehicles, SAE, 2022, pp.70–89.

[9] A. Eraliev and G. Bracco, "Design and Implementation of Zigbee Based Low-Power Wireless Sensor and Actuator Network (WSAN) for Automation of Urban Garden Irrigation Systems," 2021 IEEE International IOT, Electronics and Mechatronics Conference (IEMTRONICS), 2021, pp. 1–7. doi: 10.1109/IEMTRONICS52119.2021.9422568.

[10] N. Mishra, P. Singhal, and S. Kundu, "Application of IoT Products in Smart Cities of India," 2020 9th International Conference System Modeling and Advancement in Research Trends (SMART), pp. 155–157. doi: 10.1109/ SMART50582.2020.9337150.

[11] A. Eleyan and J. Fallon, "IoT-based Home Automation Using Android Application," 2020 International Symposium on Networks, Computers and Communications (ISNCC), 2020, pp. 1–4. doi: 10.1109/ ISNCC49221.2020.9297320.

[12] S. Wasnik and R. Venkatesh, "Understanding usage of IoT Applications and its impact on consumer decision making in Indian Automobile industry," 2022 International Conference on Decision Aid Sciences and Applications (DASA), 2022, pp. 1259–1264. doi: 10.1109/ DASA54658.2022.9765216.

[13] Saravjeet Singh and Jaiteg Singh, "Location Driven Edge Assisted Device and Solutions for Intelligent Transportation," in *Fog, Edge, and Pervasive Computing in Intelligent IoT Driven Applications*, IEEE, 2021, pp.123–147. doi: 10.1002/9781119670087.ch7.

[14] Shalli Rani, R. Maheswar, G. R. Kanagachidambaresan, Sachin Ahuja, and Deepali Gupta, *Machine Learning Paradigm for Internet of Things Applications*, John Wiley & Sons, 2022.

[15] S. Kulkarni, A. Darekar, and S. Shirol, "Proposed framework for V2V communication using Li-Fi technology," 2017 International Conference on Circuits, Controls, and Communications (CCUBE), 2017, pp. 187–190. doi: 10.1109/CCUBE.2017.8394163.

[16] G. R. Kanagachidambaresan, *Role of Single Board Computers (SBCs) in rapid IoT Prototyping*, Springer, 2021. https://doi.org/10.1007/978-3-030-72957-8.

CHAPTER 2

IoT Sensors and Their Interfacing Protocols

Sensors can detect specific entities or functions by looking for them in the environment [1]. Electromechanical, optoelectrical, or electronic equipment can all be used to create these devices. Detectors for physical presence, such as flame or metal, can be found. Others include sensors that monitor gas and chemical concentrations and other sorts of sensors. There are additional varieties that can detect motion or closeness, while others can monitor physical qualities like temperature, pressure, or radiation, for example [3].

It depends on the application [2], but electromagnetic fields, optics, or a mix of these can be used. It is common practice to employ a variety of sensors, detectors, and transducers in a wide range of industries to evaluate, monitor, and regulate machines' processes and functions. As the Internet of Things (IoT) becomes more widespread, so does the demand for sensors as the main automation tool [5]. Figure 2-1 showcases different types of sensors.

© G. R. Kanagachidambaresan 2022
G. R. Kanagachidambaresan, *Internet of Things Using Single Board Computers*,
https://doi.org/10.1007/978-1-4842-8108-6_2

SENSORS				
Sensor for contact detection	Sensors of Force	Sensors of Temperature	Sensors for Radiation	Sensors for Pressure	
	Sensors of Flow	Sensors of Position	Sensors for Photoelectric	Sensors for Particles	Sensors of electrical measurement
	Sensors of Defects	Sensors of Motion	Sensors for Metal Detectors	Sensors for Levels	
	Flame Detectors	Sensors of Leaks	Sensors for Humidity detection	Sensors for gases and chemicals	

Figure 2-1. *Types of sensors*

Vision and Imaging Sensors

Figure 2-2 shows an image based display.

Figure 2-2. *Image sensors*

The visual perception and imaging sensors/detectors [4] are electrical devices that detect the presence of objects or colors inside their fields of view and convert the data into a visual image that may be displayed. The sensor type, intended application, and any special transducer properties are all critical specifications.

Vision and imaging sensors are utilized in numerous manufacturing processes for quality control, presence detection, positioning, orientation, sorting, labeling, inspecting, gripping, and guiding, among other functions.

Touch screens for onboard programming and remote programming capabilities may or may not be incorporated into the sensors [6]. Like other sensors, they can transmit output signals to control systems that direct actions on components (or not), such as ejecting a defective package. This type of camera is often called a "smart" camera [7].

The concept of *embedded vision* comes in a variety of flavors, and it has become a buzzword in the business world. There are both black-and-white and color sensors available. Numerous tasks requiring color differentiation can be accomplished with a monochrome machine. Color processing is a very difficult task. Most sensors incorporate light rings around their lenses to appropriately illuminate the optics.

Light Rings

Sometimes, additional lighting is used. Lights can be white, red, blue, or green, depending on the imaging task. Under green light, facial abnormalities can sometimes be noticed more clearly. Backlighting can bring attention to features in a complex shape that might otherwise be overlooked in front lighting. There is also infrared and ultraviolet lighting. A variety of wide-angle and telephoto photos can be created by changing lenses. In most cases, imaging sensors are fast enough to capture photographs of products as they pass by. Other image sensing methods are used for high-speed lines like printing, such as the ones described next [9].

Shop Floor and Production Line Inspections

The sensors in the photographs can be set to identify many things [14]. A missing feature in a machined object, such as a hole or numerous holes, can be detected using an area sensor [8]. It could be used to ensure that all blister packs are filled. Blemish sensors are used in low-light conditions to detect scratches on a surface or foreign substances on packaging material and check features. Match sensors match patterns such as inscriptions to reference patterns, double-check label positioning on packages, and double-check the presence of a weld nut [11]. A sort sensor can orient a part by comparing it to multiple patterns [10]. It might also be used to ensure that a surgical kit contains all of the required components. These aren't separate sensors; they're merely distinct modes of operation for the same one. Sensors can be configured to employ any of the capturing modes.

Vision sensors are typically easy to set up and program. A reference image of a "good" part can be recorded and used by the software to compare varied areas of interest to the known good image. Dimensional data can be acquired by counting pixels, allowing you to examine the diameter of a hole or other part characteristics, for example. Many setup stages, such as focusing, are one-time actions conducted with the camera fixed in place for inspection. End-of-line inspection systems are no longer the only applications for inspection systems [12]. Systems, for example, can be used to check a correct assembly sequence at various stages of the production process [13]. As with the camera-in-the-loop example, the inspection system may flag an improper assembly, and the assembler may repair the mistake before proceeding to the next phase.

Line Scan Cameras

Figure 2-3 shows a line scan camera.

Figure 2-3. Line scan camera

Using vision sensors to check discrete parts is not the same as using them to check fast-moving products like printed webs or sheet steel in a continuous process. Some of these applications use area cameras, and the resulting images are "stitched" together in software. However, you can also use a line scan camera [15]. Using rows of pixels, these cameras are set up to take a single-line photo at the same speed as the moving object. Using downstream air jets, these cameras could be used to eliminate trash and food that isn't good enough to eat. In general, these cameras are not like regular vision sensors and need their own image processing.

3D Depth Cameras

Figure 2-4 showcases a 3D stereo vision camera.

Figure 2-4. *3D Depth cameras*

Three-dimensional cameras use stereo vision, time-of-flight, and laser triangulation to determine what a 3D image looks like. Each one has its own set of pros and cons. Laser triangulation works well in dim light and on surfaces that are hard to measure, but it is slow. Time-of-flight is a good way to measure distances and volumes and is often used in palletizing and self-driving vehicles.

Event/Production Line Triggering

Vision sensors can be set up to take pictures in several different ways. Triggering is how the sensors respond to an input by capturing and analyzing an image. An internal timer, for example, could be used by the sensor to take an image every x seconds. The sensor can be instructed to

35

take a picture based on the current state of the machine by an external source, such as a machine controller. The sensor can also be set to run indefinitely or activated by a signal sent via industrial Ethernet or manual input.

Sensors That Measure Temperature

An RTD based temperature sensor is shown in Figure 2-5.

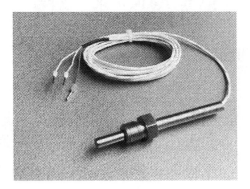

Figure 2-5. *Temperature sensors*

Transducers are electronic devices that monitor and transmit temperature data to the inputs of other devices, such as controllers and displays [16]. RTDs and thermistors are frequently used as temperature sensors because they can measure temperature and convert it to a voltaic output. The type of sensor/detector used, the maximum and minimum temperatures that can be measured, and the diameter and length of the sensor/detector are all critical specifications. Temperature sensors [18] are used in process industries to determine the thermal properties of gases, liquids, and solids.

Thermocouples

Figure 2-6 shows a thermocouple used in industries for identifying the temperature.

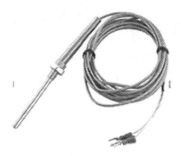

Figure 2-6. *Thermocouple*

A thermocouple uses a probe to detect the temperature by joining two different metals to make a junction on one end and connect the other end to a voltmeter [17]. The hot junction end of the probe (where the metals are connected) touches the object whose temperature is being monitored, while the cold junction end remains at a constant temperature. The voltmeter displays a potential difference in volts, proportionally indicating the temperature difference between the thermocouple's hot and cold junctures. Table 2-1 showcases the different bimetal combinations with their symbols.

Table 2-1. *Bimetal temperature sensor and their symbols*

S. No	Bimetal combination	Thermocouple
1	Iron/Constantan	J
2	Nickel-Chromium / Nickel-Alumel	K
3	Copper/Constantan	T
4	Nickel-Chromium/Constantan	E
5	Nicrosil / Nisil	N
6	Platinum Rhodium – 10% / Platinum	S
7	Platinum Rhodium –13% / Platinum	R
8	Platinum Rhodium – 30% / Platinum Rhodium – 6%	B

Resistance Temperature Detector (RTD)

An RTD is a temperature sensor that measures the electrical resistance of a conductor to estimate its temperature. Resistance is the ability of a conductor, such as a metal, to conduct electricity when a particular voltage or potential difference is applied to it. Heating a piece of metal increases its electrical conductivity, which is measured in ohms. When a little electrical current, typically 1–5 milliamps, passes through a resistive element and measures the resistance, an RTD is created. Material attributes of the resistive element can be used to translate the recorded resistance value to a temperature value. In RTDs, platinum is the metal of choice because of its excellent thermal stability, chemical inertness, and ability to function across a wide temperature range. This last aspect simplifies the process of converting electrical resistance into temperature readings. Nickel and copper can also be used as RTD resistors. The material used in RTDs is specified for its temperature coefficient of resistance (TCR). This value depicts how the electrical resistance of a material change as the temperature changes by one degree. Metals and electrically conductive materials have a positive temperature-dependent resistivity (TCR); semiconductors and non-metallic substances have a negative TCR. Figure 2-7 showcases an RTD based sensor.

Figure 2-7. *RTD sensor*

RTDs frequently utilize thin-film or wire-wound materials. For film-type RTDs, platinum is plated onto a ceramic plate and encased in glass, but for wire-wound RTDs, platinum wire is wound around a ceramic core and encased in glass. The most common wiring configurations for RTDs include two-wire, three-wire, and four-wire. Using two wires simplifies the setup but at the expense of precision, as the resistance of the wire leads cannot be differentiated from the measured resistance value. Two distinct measurements can be made using the three-wire configuration, with the wire lead resistance effect reduced from the overall resistance measurement to yield a net resistance result. Due to the four-wire arrangement, the sensor resistance can be directly measured without regard to the lead wires. A Wheatstone bridge design is frequently employed to monitor resistance in conjunction with RTDs to determine temperature values.

Temperature Thermistor Sensors

Thermistors, created from the words thermosensitive resistors, are temperature sensors that use the electrical resistance change produced by temperature to provide a reading of the temperature value. When the temperature fluctuates, a precise change in electrical resistance can be seen in these passive devices. According to their temperature coefficient, thermometers are divided into two groups: those with a negative temperature coefficient (NTC) and those with a positive temperature coefficient (PTC). A thermistor with a decreasing resistance has an NTC, whereas one with a rising temperature coefficient (PTC) has an increasing resistance. NTC and PTC thermistors are two of the most popular options in temperature sensing. Figure 2-8 showcases a temperature thermistor sensor.

Figure 2-8. *Temperature thermistor sensor*

Examples of protection applications include limiting inrush current or providing surge protection for a circuit or device. Various materials, packaging and geometries are available for thermistors depending on the temperature range and reaction time required. They can be packaged or encased in epoxy resin, glass, baked-on phenolic, or paint. Temperature sensors are typically small, inexpensive, and fast-response devices with a limited temperature range. Improved sensitivity and accuracy in readings can be achieved due to the larger change in resistance per temperature unit. The disadvantages of thermistors include that their temperature response curves are non-linear and can self-heat if the excitation current is excessively high. It is also important to note that they have a restricted temperature range and are prone to heat instability. Furthermore, the temperature curves of different manufacturers are different, making interchangeability more difficult. Temperature sensors are used in a wide variety of industries, including refrigeration, aerospace, appliances, automotive, communication, HVAC, instrumentation, medical, and military.

Semiconductor Temperature Sensors

Semiconductor temperature sensors—also called *solid-state temperature sensors*—are TO-223 and small-outline integrated circuit (SOIC) packages that are put onto printed circuit boards (PCBs). Figure 2-9 shows an SoIC based temperature sensor.

Figure 2-9. *Temperature sensors for semiconductors*

Semiconductor diodes or transistors with voltage-current characteristics that vary with temperature are used in the devices.

The following are some of the most common types of temperature sensors in semiconductors.

Temperature sensors with digital output, temperature sensors with resistance output, and temperature sensors with diode output are all examples of temperature sensors.

To get reliable data, these temperature sensors must be correctly calibrated. Although they have a wide temperature range, they cannot be used to measure extremely high temperatures.

Thermometers

This type of thermometer is non-contact and does not use an analog scale to measure temperature. It is possible to obtain a temperature reading by measuring how much black body radiation an object emits. Through a lens, a thermopile generates an electrical output proportional to the amount of heat absorbed by a thermometer. The ability to record and save data from infrared thermometers is a time-saving and process-simplifying feature. It is common practice to use an infrared thermometer to monitor the temperature of sensitive locations such as the tympanic membrane (eardrum). A further benefit for firefighters is that they can analyze the spread of a fire without manually inspecting or checking for hot spots within a burning area using thermal imaging cameras. Figure 2-10 shows an infrared based temperature identification sensor.

Figure 2-10. *Thermometers*

Because the unit can take readings without touching anything, it can also be used when direct contact with persons or equipment would be hazardous.

Radiation Sensors

Figure 2-11 showcases a radiation based sensor for identifying the temperature.

Figure 2-11. *Radiation sensor*

When alpha, beta, or gamma particles are present, radiation sensors/ detectors detect them and send an electrical signal to counters and displays. Sensor types, as well as minimum and maximum detectable energies, are all important considerations. Studies and sample counting employ radiation detectors.

Radiation detectors come in a variety of configurations.

Radiation detectors can be classified according to the type of radiation they intend to detect or their underlying operating principles. Radiation detectors are classified functionally as counters, spectrometers, and radiation dosimeters.

The following are the most frequently used types of radiation detectors.

- Radiation detectors with a gaseous filling

- Detectors of scintillation radiation

- Detectors of radiation using solid-state technology

Proximity Sensors

Figure 2-12 showcases a proximity sensor for position recognition.

Figure 2-12. *Proximity sensor*

Proximity sensors [20] are electronic devices that can tell when something is close without touching it. A proximity sensor can find things within a few centimeters and send a DC output signal to a controller. In many manufacturing processes, proximity sensors are used to find nearby items and machine parts. Important factors include the type of sensor, its maximum sensing distance, minimum and maximum working temperatures, and length and diameter. Most proximity sensors have a short range, but some can pick up on things up to a few inches away. A capacitive proximity sensor shows this type of sensor. This device detects a change in capacitance caused by a decrease in the distance between the plates of a capacitor, one of which is attached to the object under observation. This change in capacitance is caused by a decrease in the distance between the capacitor plates. The sensor can then tell how the object is moving and where it is.

There are different kinds of proximity sensors, and each has its own way of working.

Inductive Field Sensors

Inductive proximity sensors are the greatest way to detect ferrous metals, particularly steel thicker than 1 mm. These sensors produce a magnetic field interrupted by metal, alerting the sensor to its presence. Shielded inductive sensors are used to add metal to the field in a controlled manner because any metal, even the metal in which the sensor is embedded, affects the sensor. This enables the sensor to detect anomalies in the field as new metal bits pass by and limits the sensor's range. Non-shielded sensors offer a greater range but cannot be put on or near ferrous metal.

Magnetic Field Sensors

Figure 2-13 showcases the magnetic field sensors.

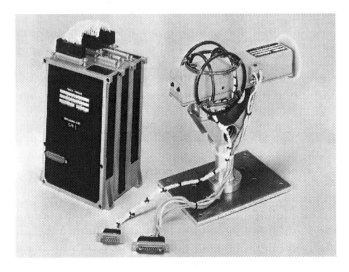

Figure 2-13. *Magnetometer*

Magnetic proximity [19] sensors can detect magnets through nonferrous metals, plastic, and wood, making them helpful in clean-in-place (CIP) systems for tracking cleaning equipment inside pipelines. In these sensors, a hermetically sealed reed switch detects adjacent magnets. When a magnet is present, the reed contacts stretch and make contact with one another, producing an electrical contact and alerting the system to the presence of a magnet.

Light Sensors/Photodetectors

Figure 2-14 showcases a light sensor and photo detector.

Figure 2-14. *Photosensitive light sensor*

Photoelectric proximity sensors are ideal for usage in environments such as conveyor belts and automatic sinks and in the presence of dense air pollutants. Photoelectric sensors transmit visible or invisible light to a receiver and notify the system if it is blocked. They are available in dark-on and light-on configurations, with the system alerted when no light is detected or when light is received.

They are classified into three types.

- Through-beam sensors have a receiver on one side of the area to be sensed and an emitter on the other. These photoelectric sensors are the most dependable but also the most expensive. They can be fooled by more transparent or lighter-colored things that the beam can pass through.

- Retro-reflective sensors retain the emitter and receiver in the same spot by using a reflector on the opposite side of the region to be detected. These are less expensive and quicker to install, but they can be deceived by shiny items passing through the beam.

- In diffuse sensors, the detected object acts as a reflector. While they are obstructed by less reflecting targets, such as dark matte materials, they can discriminate between darker and lighter materials, making them ideal for sorting.

Types of Photoelectric Sensors

Although they are all based on the same principle, photoelectric sensors operate somewhat differently depending on their structure, resulting in varied advantages and disadvantages. Through-beam photoelectric sensors are the third most common form of sensor.

In diffuse photoelectric sensors, the emitter and receiver are one unit. The sensor's light is reflected to the receiver, alerting the system that something has passed through its path. These sensors are the most difficult to install because of their sensitivity to variations in surface texture, color, and other environmental conditions. Multiple and transparent objects, container fill levels, object orientation, and undesired situations can all be detected by using these devices.

Like diffuse photoelectric transmitters, retro-reflective photoelectric transmitters employ a mirror in front of them to reflect light to the receiver instead of emitting it. Objects passing in front of a sensor's mirror notify the system of the missing signal. Through-beam sensors are more accurate than diffused sensors and easier to install than diffused sensors for transparent, big, and shiny objects and moving objects.

Through-beam photoelectric sensors have a secondary receiver located across from the transmitter. The system is only alerted when an object interrupts the signal between the transmitter and receiver. In terms of precision and range, these sensors top the list. However, they must be in two sections and can't operate in dirty conditions. They'll pick up on it if they're not too big or too small or too thick or too thin or too long.

Ultrasonic Proximity Sensors

An ultrasonic proximity sensor is often employed in automated production. It can detect the presence of dark or light objects such as glass from a distance, fluid levels, and stacks of paper and wood. They can also be used to reduce noise. These sensors utilize transducer-pulsed sound waves, available in the same through-beam, retro-reflective, and diffuse types as photoelectric sensors. Ultrasonic sensors can be harmed by unusual textures, resulting in distorted sound.

Pressure Sensors

Figure 2-15 showcases an array based pressure sensor.

Figure 2-15. *Pressure sensor*

Electromechanical devices called *pressure sensors* [19], detectors, and transducers can be used to measure forces per unit area in gases and liquids. Pressure sensors and transducers often use a diaphragm and a strain gauge bridge to determine how much force is being put on a unit area. Important specs describe how the sensor works, its minimum and maximum operating pressures, and its full-scale accuracy. Pressure sensors control or measure things that need to know how much pressure gas or liquid has.

Position Sensors

Figure 2-16 illustrates the position sensors.

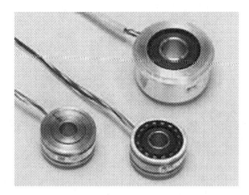

Figure 2-16. *Position sensors*

These electronic devices sense the position of valves, doors, throttles, etc., and provide signals to the control or display devices. It is critical to consider the various types, functionalities, measurement ranges, and sensor-specific features available. Control applications that require precise location information can benefit from positioning sensors [21]. One of the most prevalent position sensors is the string potentiometer.

Photoelectric Sensors

Figure 2-17 shows the photoelectric sensors.

Figure 2-17. *Photoelectric sensors*

Objects traveling through the detecting area are detected using photoelectric sensors, which are electrical devices that can detect color, cleanliness, and location if necessary. These sensors use an emitter and a receiver to detect fluctuations in light output. Automated counting, robot picking, and doors and gates are examples of how they are used in the manufacturing and material handling industries.

Particle Sensors

Dust and other airborne particulates are detected by sensors/detectors, which provide signals to control and display inputs. The employment of particle sensors [22] to monitor containers and baghouses is commonplace. Transducer type, minimum detectable particle size, and operational temperature range are critical specifications. In nuclear engineering, particle detectors are used to detect radiation.

Types of Particle Sensors

Solid, liquid, and aerosol particle sensors fall into one of these three major groups. This chapter explains how they work and how they are put to good use.

Aerosol Particle Sensors

Figure 2-18 illustrates a particle sensor.

Figure 2-18. *Aerosol sensor*

The quality of the air is determined by the amount and size of aerosol particles in the air. Particle count in a building or the surrounding air can be estimated using this information. Furthermore, it helps to understand the level of cleanliness in a controlled environment. In clean rooms, aerosol particle sensors are commonly employed. Among other industries, clean rooms are utilized in semiconductor manufacturing, biotechnology, pharmaceutics, and optical disc drive manufacturing. In clean rooms, the number of particles per cubic meter is regulated. Aerosol particle counters or sensors ensure that a cleanroom satisfies regulatory standards.

Solid Particle Sensors

Figure 2-19 showcases a particulate matter sensor.

Figure 2-19. *Dust sensor*

Detection of the size of dry particles can be accomplished with solid particle sensors. It can determine how much material comes from a rock crusher at a quarry. Sieves are the most commonly used method in the industry to measure the size of dry particles. The size of dry particles can also be determined using vision-based methods. Particle sizing can be done quickly and precisely using a vision-based method.

Liquid Particle Sensors

Figure 2-20 shows an IR based turbidity sensor for liquid turbidity identification.

Figure 2-20. *Turbidity sensor*

The quality of any fluid can be determined via liquid particle sensors. This information helps testers determine if the liquid is clean enough for the intended application. For example, liquid particle counters can be used to determine the quality of drinking water or cleaning solutions and to inspect power generation equipment or injectable medicines for cleanliness.

Fluid particle counters also monitor hydraulic fluid cleanliness and systems like engines and gears. Hydraulic breakdowns are likely caused by contamination in 75% to 80% of the cases. A wide variety of sensors can be employed on equipment, in a laboratory for oil analysis, or on a machine at the job site to verify fluid purity. Hydraulic failures can be minimized, uptime and machine availability increased, and oil consumption lowered by identifying and monitoring these levels and following a maintenance program. Hydraulic fluids can be checked for appropriate cleanliness levels using particle monitoring after they have been cleaned with filtration.

Metal Detectors

Figure 2-21 shows an RF based metal detector.

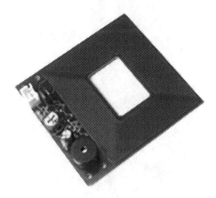

Figure 2-21. *Metal detector*

Electronic or electromechanical metal detectors can detect metal in many scenarios, from parcels to people. Permanent or portable metal detectors can use various sensor technologies, the most common of which is electromagnetic, to detect metal. As a result, a wide range of options is available, such as handheld or fixed devices and a range of detecting distances. For example, metal detectors can be tailored to detect metal during sawmilling or injection molding.

Level Sensors

Figure 2-22 shows a level detection sensor.

Figure 2-22. *Level sensor*

Level sensors and detectors are electrical or electromechanical devices that send signals to control or display devices in tanks or bins to measure the height of gases, liquids, or solids and send the information to the right equipment. Most level sensors use ultrasonic, capacitance, vibratory, or mechanical methods to determine a product's height. The type of sensor, how it works, and the maximum distance it can sense are all important things to consider. There are two main kinds of level sensors and detectors: those that don't touch the liquid and those that do.

Leak Detectors

Figure 2-23 shows a leak detection sensor.

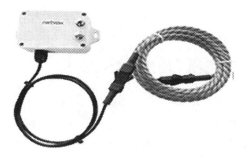

Figure 2-23. *Leak sensor*

Sensors and detectors for liquid and gas leak detection and monitoring are electronic equipment [23]. Ultrasonic technology, for example, can detect air leaks in some leak detectors. Other leak detectors use simple foaming agents to test the soundness of pipe junctions. Vacuum package seals can be tested using other leak detectors.

Humidity Sensors

Figure 2-24 shows the DHT11 temperature and humidity sensor.

Figure 2-24. *Humidity sensor*

Humidity sensors, detectors, and transducers are electrical devices that can operate or display various types of equipment by measuring and converting the amount of water in the air into signals. In addition to the lowest and highest operating temperatures, response time is a significant feature.

Gas and Chemical Sensors

Fixed or portable electronic devices, known as sensors/detectors for gases and chemicals, are used to detect the presence and properties of gases and chemicals. A sensor's or detector's type, range, and features are important considerations. In confined space monitoring, leak detection, and analytical instrumentation, gas and chemical sensors/detectors are often utilized and are often built to detect several gases and chemicals.

Gas Detectors

Figure 2-25 showcases the gas detection MQ sensor.

Figure 2-25. *Gas sensor*

Gas sensors and detectors [24] are used in many applications, from flammable gases in industrial plants to ethanol in breathalyzer tests, to detect the presence of gases. The most common gas sensors are made of metal oxides and can detect a wide range of gases, including butane and hydrogen. MQ detectors come in multiple shapes and sizes. Methane and butane, for example, are detected by MQ2 sensors. MQ138 sensors detect benzene and toluene.

A tin oxide-coated ceramic element is at the heart of an MQ2 sensor. The tin oxide emits free electrons when the element is heated. These electrons combine with oxygen, causing no current to flow through the sensor. Some electrons remain uncombined with oxygen as the atmosphere changes due to the presence of butane, for example, and a small current flows through the sensor. More current flows through the device as the amount of oxygen decreases, providing a quantifiable measure of the amount of gas in the atmosphere. The sensor element is usually encased in mesh to keep dust out and prevent flammable gases from igniting the element's heating. MQ2 methane, butane, LPG; MQ3 methane, butane, LPG; MQ4 methane; MQ3 ethanol, Butane; and MQ6 LPG are some MQ series sensors.

Carbon Monoxide (MQ7) Detectors

In addition to bare sensors and modules, MQ sensors can be purchased in various combinations. The modules have op-amp comparators and digital output pins to identify the presence of gases. The naked sensor is connected to a microprocessor to obtain a precise gas concentration reading (measured in parts per million, or ppm).

Non-dispersive infrared detection is a sensor technique that determines the spectrum of an air sample by using infrared light and a waveguide packaged on a small platform. CO_2 monitoring in HVAC and indoor air monitoring applications is the primary application for these sensors. PID (photoionization detection) is another method for detecting the presence of volatile organic compounds like ketones and aromatics. PID detectors ionize gas with high-energy UV light, resulting in a current proportional to the amount of VOCs (volatile organic compounds) in the atmosphere.

Force Sensors

Figure 2-26 showcases an array based force sensor.

Figure 2-26. *Force sensor*

They are digital devices that measure parameters connected with forces such as weight, torque, load, and so on and send signals to control or display devices' inputs. Force sensors/transducers [25]. Force sensors are typically built around a piezoelectric load cell, a device that alters its resistance in response to deforming stresses. Torque and strain can be measured in multiple ways. As a result, these criteria are critical: sensor function, number of axes, minimum and maximum loads (or torques), working temperatures, and sensor dimensions. Force sensors are employed in a wide range of applications, from truck scales to bolt tensioning devices, to determine the weight of materials.

Force Sensor Types

A wide variety of force sensors exist, each of which uses a different technology to determine the amount of a given force and produce an output signal. Of all force sensors, load cells and strain gauges are the most utilized (FSRs).

A variety of load cells may be used to measure compressive forces, most often weight, by converting the applied force to an output signal. If you need a load cell, you can choose from a wide selection because they can provide an output utilizing different technologies.

- Load cells pneumatic

- Hydraulic force sensors

- Load cells based on piezoelectric crystals

- Load cells that are inductive

- Cells de charge capacitive sensors

- Load cells with magnetostrictive properties

- Load cells with strain gauge

Flow Sensors

Figure 2-27 shows a simple generator based water flow sensor/meter.

Figure 2-27. *Flow sensor*

Electrical or electromechanical flow sensors/detectors can send signals to other devices to regulate or show the inputs of such devices. You can use ultrasonic detection from outside the pipeline or a paddlewheel that sits and spins directly in the flow stream as a flow sensor. You can even combine the two. Flow rate, working pressure, and minimum and maximum operating temperatures are all critical criteria for a sensor/ detector. Flow sensors [26] are frequently utilized in the manufacturing business. Allowing process operators to quickly see flow conditions is a benefit of some panel mounting designs.

There are three flow sensor classifications.

- Flow sensors that detect positive displacement

- Mass flow monitoring sensors

- Sensors that measure flow velocity

Positive displacement flow sensors are distinct from other flow sensors in that they directly measure the fluid volume moving through the instrument. Other flow sensors monitor different characteristics (such as pressure) and use that information to calculate or infer the flow rate. A positive displacement flow sensor captures and delivers a known quantity of fluid by spinning elements that successfully transfer this fluid consecutively before allowing more fluid to enter the device.

In some ways, the procedure resembles continually filling and emptying a water pail. As the rotating components complete a full rotation, a known volume of fluid flows through the sensor. Calculate the amount of fluid passed per unit of time by calculating the number of revolutions. Since the fluid flow directly moves the rotating components, the rotational velocity is proportional to the flow rate.

Mechanical seals confine the fluid within the flow sensor, preventing any fluid from bypassing or slipping past the device without being measured. The precision of positive displacement flow sensors is limited only by the degree of slippage due to high-quality components with small clearances. In addition, they may be able to operate with a wide variety of fluid viscosities, require minimal maintenance, and feature a mechanical or electrical interface. Oil, gasoline, hydraulic fluid, and domestic water and gas metering are a few examples.

Mass Flow Sensors

Figure 2-28 shows a mass fluid flow sensor.

Figure 2-28. *Mass flow sensor*

Mass flow sensors, also known as *mass air flow sensors,* are commonly used in automotive applications to measure the mass of air entering an engine's air intake system. Electronic engine control uses the sensor's output to calculate how much fuel to feed the engine to achieve the correct fuel-air mixture for ignition.

Mass flow sensors measure energy transmission from a heated surface to a flowing fluid. One method involves injecting a given amount of thermal energy and watching the temperature change. In contrast, the other involves maintaining a constant temperature for a probe and estimating the amount of thermal energy required. A hot wire mass flow sensor is a device that consists of a resistive wire connected to temperature sensors through electric current. Convective heat transfer lowers the wire's electrical resistance as the airflow past the sensor increases. The electrical current required to maintain the temperature of the hot wire increases as the resistance decreases, allowing the electrical current required to maintain the temperature of the hot wire to be utilized as a mass flow rate measurement. Temperature differences can be used to determine mass flow rates in other ways.

The Coriolis flow meter is another type of mass flow sensor. As the fluid moves through an oscillating tube, the inertia causes twisting in the tube, which is directly proportional to the fluid's mass flow rate, according to this mass flow meter's hypothesis. Using a driving coil, two tubes in the sensor vibrate at opposite resonance frequencies to separate and direct the process fluid. Electronic sensors in the tubes convert the oscillations into a sine wave as they occur. No flow means that the entrance and outflow sinusoids are in phase, indicating that the tubes are moving step by step.

The Coriolis force causes the tubes to bend in the opposite direction as fluid flows through them. In response to this motion, the sine waves alter in phase, indicating that the two tubes are moving at different rates.

In fluid flow, the time difference between two sine waves, given by the symbol t, directly correlates to the mass flow rate. If you know how many sine waves there are, you can figure out how dense the fluid in the tubes is. On the other hand, the density of the fluid is directly related to the square of the frequency. Denser fluids have a lower frequency of oscillation. When the mass flow rate and fluid density are known, volumetric flow can be easily calculated.

Velocity Flow Sensors

Figure 2-29 shows a velocity flow sensor.

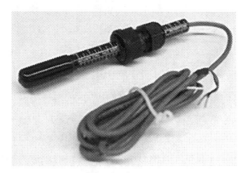

Figure 2-29. *Velocity flow sensor*

Flow rate is calculated using a velocity flow sensor, which measures a fluid's velocity as it travels past the sensor. The velocity flow sensor is available in many shapes and sizes, such as the following.

- Mechanism-based (e.g., turbine, propeller, and paddle wheel)

- Electromagnetic

- Ultrasonic

With mechanical flow sensors, a spinning mechanical component, such as a paddle wheel mounted on a bearing, extends from the sensor and rests in the flow channel. Hall effect, magnetic coil, and infrared sensors detect the rotation of the paddle wheel in response to fluid flow. The flow sensor's electronics convert the rotations into an output signal, such as a rectangular wave pulse, that can be set to represent a certain volume output per unit time.

Paddle wheel flow sensors are inexpensive, have a straightforward operating principle, are compact, and consume very little electricity. These sensors are also compatible with many fluid types because their operation is not dependent on conductive fluid. One of the sensor's downsides is the inclusion of moving parts, which are susceptible to wear and contamination by unclean fluids, obstructing performance and necessitating maintenance. Paddle wheel flow sensors require a minimum flow rate to function properly; otherwise, the device would be useless.

Electromatic flow sensors (also known as *EMF flow sensors* and *magnetic flow sensors*) are governed by Faraday's law of induction. Before measuring the voltage created by the conductive fluid passing through the magnetic field, the devices use a coil to create a magnetic field in the fluid under inquiry. The fluid velocity in the pipe determines the induced voltage. The velocity data can be converted to a volumetric flow rate if the pipe's cross-sectional dimensions are known.

Electromagnetic flow sensors require a minimum conductivity in the monitored fluid and do not cause a reduction in pipe pressure. They are effective against polluted fluids, not non-conductive fluids such as oil, steam, or gas. Fluids likely to coat the electrodes should be avoided while utilizing this type of sensor, as the electrodes can become coated. Vacuum, abrasive fluids, and fluids containing ferromagnetic particles are incompatible with magnetic flow sensors.

Ultrasonic flow sensors monitor flow using two alternative methods. In the initial approach, a pair of ultrasonic transducers produce a signal focused in both directions into the fluid flow. A pair of mirrors reflect each signal emitted by a transmitter to the receiver of the other transducer. For a portion of its journey, one signal travels in the direction of the fluid flow while the other travels in the opposite direction.

By measuring the transit periods of the two signals, the receiver electronics determine the time difference between them. While the fluid is stationary, the transit times of both signals are identical; however, when the fluid is moving, the signal traveling with the flow has a shorter transit time. Thus, the difference in the two signals' transit times represents the fluid velocity. Transit time ultrasonic flow sensors are another name for these ultrasonic flow sensors.

Flaw Sensors

Figure 2-30 shows an ultrasonic based flaw detection sensor.

Figure 2-30. *Flaw sensor*

Flaw sensors and detectors are electronic devices used in many industrial processes to find flaws on surfaces or in materials underneath, like welds. Flaw detectors are systems that use ultrasonic, acoustic, or other means to find flaws in materials. They can be portable or fixed. The type of sensor, the range of faults or thicknesses that can be seen, and the application are all important things to think about.

Flame Detectors

Figure 2-31 shows an IR based flame detection sensor.

Figure 2-31. *Flame sensor*

These devices are electronic devices that detect the presence and kind of fire and provide signals to control devices' inputs, such as smoke and heat detectors. A UV or infrared flame detector can be utilized in many combustion control applications, including burners. When choosing a detector, the type matters; under-the-hood fire suppression systems, for example, make extensive use of flame detectors.

Voltmeter and Ammeter Sensors

Current, voltage, and other variables can be detected by electrical devices, which then send signals to control devices or visual displays. Hall effect detection is extensively employed in electrical sensors, but other approaches are also used. These parameters include the sensor's type and purpose, as well as the sensor's minimum and maximum measurement ranges and operating temperature ranges. Electrical sensors are used in anything from railway systems to fan, pump, and heater monitoring to acquire information about the condition of electrical systems.

Contact Sensors

Figure 2-32 showcases a contact sensor.

Figure 2-32. *Contact sensor*

A contact sensor is any sensor that detects a state by physical contact between the sensor and an item. A simple touch sensor monitors doors, windows, and other access points. A magnetic switch that sends a signal to the alarm control unit when the door or window is closed can determine the condition of the door or window. When a door or window is opened, a contact sensor that informs the controller of the access point's condition may activate an audio siren. Contact sensors are used in robotics and other automated machinery for temperature monitoring and proximity sensing.

Non-Contact Sensors

Figure 2-33 showcases a non-contact sensor.

Figure 2-33. *Non-contact sensor*

Unlike contact sensors, non-contact sensors do not require physical contact between the sensor and the monitored object to the function. Motion detectors, such as those seen in security lights, are examples of this type of sensor. Non-mechanical or non-physical technologies such as passive infrared energy, microwave radiation, ultrasonic waves, and others are used to detect objects within the range of a motion detector. Radar guns, employed by law enforcement to monitor vehicle speeds, are another non-contact sensor. Hall effect sensors, inductive sensors, LVDTs (linear variable differential transformers), RVDTs (rotary variable differential transformers), and eddy current sensors are non-contact.

Sensor Communication Protocols

Figure 2-34 showcases the different communication protocols between processors.

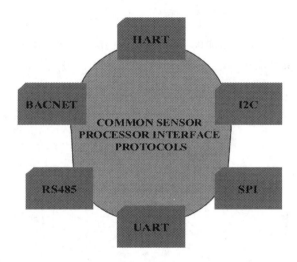

Figure 2-34. *Communication protocols*

Summary

Sensor classification was discussed in this chapter. Wired interfacing with SBCs was also covered. Programming sensors and interfacing with Python is discussed in the next chapter.

References

[1] Jeffrey Wishart, Yan Chen, Steven Como, Narayanan Kidambi, Duo Lu, and Yezhou Yang, "Sensor and Actuator Hardware," *Fundamentals of Connected and Automated Vehicles*, SAE, 2022, pp. 70–89.

[2] N. Mishra, P. Singhal, and S. Kundu, "Application of IoT Products in Smart Cities of India," 2020 9th International Conference System Modeling and Advancement in Research Trends (SMART), 2020, pp. 155–157. doi: 10.1109/SMART50582.2020.9337150

[3] Nayla Omer, "Water Quality Parameters," in *Water Quality: Science, Assessments and Policy*, IntechOpen, 2020. doi:10.5772/intechopen.89657.

[4] Changhan Yoon and Changho Lee, "Recent Advances in Imaging Sensors and Applications," *Sensors*, vol. 21, 2021, pp. 3970. doi:10.3390/s21123970.

[5] Mohd Javaid, Abid Haleem, Ravi Pratap Singh, Shanay Rab, and Rajiv Suman, "Significance of sensors for industry 4.0: Roles, capabilities, and applications," *Sensors International*, vol. 2, 2021. `https://doi.org/10.1016/j.sintl.2021.100110`.

[6] J. Kim, H. Lim, S. Han, Y. Jung, and S. Lee, "Compensation Algorithm for Misrecognition Caused by Hard Pressure Touch in Plastic Cover Capacitive Touch Screen Panels," *Journal of Display Technology*, vol. 12, no. 12, Dec. 2016, pp. 1623–1628. doi: 10.1109/JDT.2016.2615678.

[7] M. O. Ali, M. M. Alam, M. F. Ahmed, and Y. M. Jang, "A New Smart-Meter Data Monitoring System based on Optical Camera Communication," 2021 International Conference on Artificial Intelligence in Information and Communication (ICAIIC), 2021, pp. 477–479. doi: 10.1109/ICAIIC51459.2021.9415233.

[8] I. Jahan, M. O. Ali, M. H. Rahman, B. Chung, and Y. M. Jang, "Vision Anomaly Detection Using Self-Gated Rectified Linear Unit," 2022 International Conference on Artificial Intelligence in Information and Communication (ICAIIC), 2022, pp. 200–203. doi: 10.1109/ICAIIC54071.2022.9722663.

[9] W. Qiao, L. Shen, J. Wang, Y. Cao, S. He, and Y. Dai, "A Fine-Grained Fully Convolutional Network for Extraction of Building Along High-Speed Rail Lines from VHR Remote Sensing Image," IGARSS 2019 – 2019 IEEE International Geoscience and Remote Sensing Symposium, 2019, pp. 1244–1247. doi: 10.1109/IGARSS.2019.8899095.

[10] P. P. Ray, S. Pradhan, R. K. Sharma, A. Rasaily, A. Swaraj, and A. Pradhan, "IoT based fruit quality measurement system," 2016 Online International Conference on Green Engineering and Technologies (IC-GET), 2016, pp. 1–5. doi: 10.1109/GET.2016.7916620.

[11] J. Baum, F. Otto, J. Kauper, T. Klein, and C. Schumann, "Fault analysis and correction by applying process-integrated measurement in automated production facilities," 2017 International Conference on Engineering, Technology and Innovation (ICE/ITMC), 2017, pp. 888–893. doi: 10.1109/ICE.2017.8279977.

[12] H. Zhong, Z. Ling, C. Miao, W. Guo, and P. Tang, "A New Robot-Based System for In-Pipe Ultrasonic Inspection of Pressure Pipelines," 2017 Far East NDT New Technology & Application Forum (FENDT), 2017, pp. 246–250. doi: 10.1109/FENDT.2017.8584579.

[13] W. Grzechca, "Assembly line balancing problem with quality inspection stations," 2015 IEEE 7th International Conference on Cybernetics and Intelligent Systems (CIS) and IEEE Conference on Robotics, Automation and Mechatronics (RAM), 2015, pp. 89–94. doi: 10.1109/ICCIS.2015.7274602.

[14] W. Baek and D. Y. Kim, "In-Process Noise Inspection System for Product Fault Detection in a Loud Shop-Floor Environment," *IEEE Transactions on Instrumentation and Measurement*, vol. 70, 2021, pp. 1–11. doi: 10.1109/TIM.2021.3061269.

[15] A. S. Saragih, F. Aditya and W. Ahmed, "Defect Identification and Measurement using Stereo Vision Camera for In-Line Inspection of Pipeline," 2022 Advances in Science and Engineering Technology International Conferences (ASET), 2022, pp. 1–5. doi: 10.1109/ASET53988.2022.9735082.

[16] I. Stoev, S. Zaharieva, and A. Borodzhieva, "Internet of Things (IoT) Application for Temperature Control in Residential Premises," 2022 21st International Symposium INFOTEH-JAHORINA (INFOTEH), 2022, pp. 1–5. doi: 10.1109/INFOTEH53737.2022.9751289.

[17] Y. Karan and S. Kahveci, "Wireless measurement of thermocouple with microcontroller," 2015 23rd Signal Processing and Communications Applications Conference (SIU), 2015, pp. 120–123. doi: 10.1109/SIU.2015.7129867.

[18] Silvano Donati, "Thermal Detectors and Thermography," in *Photodetectors: Devices, Circuits and Applications*, IEEE, 2021, pp. 245–263. doi: 10.1002/9781119769958.ch8.

[19] W. Zhang, Q. Guo, Y. Duan, C. Xing, and Z. Peng, "A Textile Proximity/Pressure Dual-Mode Sensor Based on Magneto-Straining and Piezoresistive Effects," *IEEE Sensors Journal*, vol. 22, no. 11, June 1, 2022, pp. 10420–10427. doi: 10.1109/JSEN.2022.3168068.

[20] B. Bury, "Proximity sensing for robots," *IEE Colloquium on Robot Sensors*, 1991, pp. 3/1–318.

[21] M. Sun, Y. Wang, W. Joseph, and D. Plets, "Indoor Localization Using Mind Evolutionary Algorithm-Based Geomagnetic Positioning and Smartphone IMU Sensors," *IEEE Sensors Journal*, vol. 22, no. 7, April 1, 2022, pp. 7130–7141. doi: 10.1109/JSEN.2022.3155817.

[22] R. Jia, L. Wang, C. Zheng, and T. Chen, "Online Wear Particle Detection Sensors for Wear Monitoring of Mechanical Equipment—A Review," in *IEEE Sensors Journal*, vol. 22, no. 4, Feb. 15, 2022, pp. 2930–2947. doi: 10.1109/JSEN.2021.3131467.

[23] M. L. Vinogradov, D. K. Kostrin, M. V. Karganov, and V. Y. Tiskovich, "How to choose a leak detection method," 2016 IEEE NW Russia Young Researchers in Electrical and Electronic Engineering Conference (EIConRusNW), 2016, pp. 100–104. doi: 10.1109/EIConRusNW.2016.7448130.

[24] Jun Jiang and Guoming Ma, "Dissolved Gases Detection with Optical Methods," in *Optical Sensing in Power Transformers*, IEEE, 2021, pp. 65–135. doi: 10.1002/9781119765325.ch4.

[25] C. Liu and H. Li, "Design and Experimental Validation of Novel Force Sensor," *IEEE Sensors Journal*, vol. 15, no. 8, Aug. 2015, pp. 4402–4408. doi: 10.1109/JSEN.2015.2418331.

[26] Z. Fang, X. Xu, Izhar, L. Zhang, Y. Yang, and W. Xu, "An Electrochemical Impedance-Based Flexible Flow Sensor with Ultra-Low Limit of Detection," in *IEEE Sensors Journal*, vol. 22, no. 2, Jan. 15, 2022, pp. 1180–1187. doi: 10.1109/JSEN.2021.3131669.

CHAPTER 3

Programming SBCs

A sensor is a device that detects the presence of a specific entity or function. A device can be electrical, optoelectrical, or electronic and made of specialty electronics or other sensitive materials [1,2]. Transducers are available to detect the physical presence, such as flame or metal. Other sensors include those that measure levels or detect gas and chemical presence. Some types detect motion or proximity, while others measure physical properties like temperature, pressure, or radiation. Depending on the application, they can use electromagnetic fields, optics, or a combination. Sensors, detectors, and transducers of various kinds are used in numerous applications across a wide range of industries to test, measure, and control multiple machine processes and functions as the Internet of Things (IoT) grows in popularity. Figure 3-1 shows the I^2C NodeMCU communication protocol.

© G. R. Kanagachidambaresan 2022
G. R. Kanagachidambaresan, *Internet of Things Using Single Board Computers*,
https://doi.org/10.1007/978-1-4842-8108-6_3

Arduino Programming

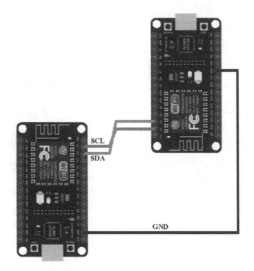

Figure 3-1. *I²C NodeMCU communication protocol*

```
//Master code
#include <Wire.h>
void setup() {
  wire.begin();
   serial.begin(9600);
}

void loop() {
  wire.requestFrom(8, 6);

  while (wire.available()) {
    char c = Wire.read();
    serial.print(c);
  }
  delay(500);
}
```

```
//Slave code
#include <Wire.h>

void setup() {
  wire.begin(8);
  wire.onRequest(requestEvent);
}

void loop() {
  delay(100);
}
```

Raspberry Pi

Raspberry Pi is a single-board computer with a small form factor. Connecting the Raspberry Pi to peripherals such as a keyboard, mouse, and display can function as a mini personal computer. Raspberry Pi is a popular platform for real-time image/video processing, IoT applications, and robotics.

While the Raspberry Pi is slower than a laptop or desktop computer, it is still a computer capable of providing all the expected features or capabilities while consuming little power.

Raspbian OS is officially provided by the Raspberry Pi Foundation and is based on Debian. Additionally, they offer the NOOBS OS for the Raspberry Pi. There are a variety of third-party operating systems, such as Ubuntu, Arch Linux, RISC OS, and Windows 10 IoT Core.

Raspbian OS is an open source operating system that is available for free use. This operating system is optimally optimized for use with the Raspberry Pi. Raspbian includes a graphical user interface (GUI) that includes tools for browsing, Python programming, office, and gaming.

You should store the OS on an SD card (a minimum of 16 GB is recommended) (operating system). Raspberry Pi is more than a computer because it gives developers access to the on-chip hardware, specifically the general-purpose input/output (GPIO). You can connect and control devices such as LEDs, motors, and sensors via GPIO. It has a Broadcom processor SoC based on ARM and an on-chip GPU (graphics processing unit).

The Raspberry Pi's CPU speed ranges from 700 MHz to 1.2 GHz. Additionally, it features onboard SDRAM ranging from 256 MB to 1 GB. Additionally, the Raspberry Pi includes on-chip SPI, I²C, I2S, and UART modules.

The Raspberry Pi is available in the following models.

- Model 3B+

- Model 42 GB

- Model 4 4GB

- Model 4 8GB

- Model Pi Zero

- Model Pi Zero W

- Model Pi Zero WH

Introduction to Raspberry Pi GPIO Access

GPIO pins can be used as inputs or outputs, which enables the Raspberry Pi to communicate with other general-purpose I/O devices.

The Raspberry Pi 3 model B removed 26 GPIO pins from the board. These GPIOs enable the Raspberry Pi to control a wide variety of external I/O devices. These pins serve as a physical link between the Raspberry Pi and the rest of the world. You can program these pins to communicate with external devices. For instance, if you want to read the state of a physical switch, you can assign any of the available GPIO pins as an input and use the switch status to make decisions. Additionally, you can configure any GPIO pin as an output to control an LED's on/off state. The Raspberry Pi can connect to the Internet via its built-in Wi-Fi or a Wi-Fi USB adapter. Once the Raspberry Pi is connected to the Internet, you can remotely control the devices connected to it.

The Raspberry Pi 3's GPIO pinout is depicted in Figure 3-2.

GPIO pins on the Raspberry Pi 3 BCertain model's GPIO pins are multiplexed to perform alternate functions such as I²C, SPI, and UART. F.

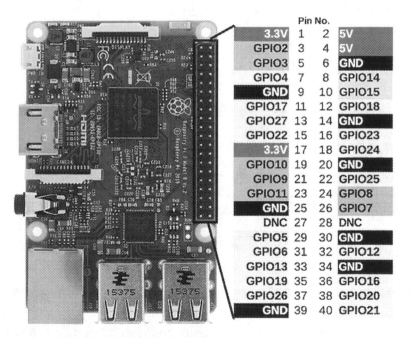

Figure 3-2. *Raspberry Pi 3's GPIO pinout*

Let's define the GPIO pins used as output or input. Raspberry Pi has two distinct methods for defining pin numbers: *GPIO numbering* and *physical numbering*.

In GPIO numbering, the term *pin number* refers to the location of a pin on a Broadcom SoC (system-on-chip). As a result, when using GPIO pins, you should always consider pin mapping.

While the pin number refers to the pin on the 40-pin P1 header on the Raspberry Pi board in physical numbering. The physical numbering scheme is straightforward, as you can simply count the pins on the P1 header and assign them to GPIO.

Now, let's control the LED using Raspberry Pi's switch. Here, you use Python and C (WiringPi) to control the LEDs' ON/OFF state.

Now, let's use Python on the Raspberry Pi to turn on and off an LED. The switch turns the LED on and off.

```
#import RPi.GPIO as GPIO
LED = 32 pins as specified on the BOARD, GPIO18 as specified
on the BCM
Switch input = 29 #pins as specified on the BOARD, GPIO27 as
specified on the BCM GPIO
setwarnings(False)
#disable GPIO warnings.
setmode(GPIO.BOARD)
# initialize the GPIO pin numbering format.
setup(LED, GPIO.OUT)
```

To use Raspberry Pi's GPIO pins in Python, you must import the RPi. GPIO package, which contains GPIO-controlling classes. On Raspbian OS, the RPi.GPIO Python package is already installed. As a result, there is no need to install it externally. Simply put, you should include a library in our program to enable us to use Python functions for GPIO access. This is detailed next.

The value of a GPIO pin is read using this function; for example, how the GPIO pins are used in BCM and BOARD modes in the RPi package is as follows.

In BCM,

       GPIO.setmode(GPIO.BCM)

       GPIO.setup(21, GPIO.OUT)

In BOARD,

         GPIO.setmode(GPIO.BOARD)

         GPIO.setup(40, GPIO.OUT)

The following is a C-based control example program.

```
#include <wiringPi.h>
#include <stdio.h>
int LED = 26;                      /*  wiringPi - GPIO26, GPIO12-
BCM, 32 pin number */
int switch_input = 21;             /*  wiringPi -GPIO21, GPIO5 -
BCM, 29 Pin number */
int main(){
     wiringPiSetup();               /* initialize setup*/
     pinMode(LED,OUTPUT);           /* configuring as output */
     pullUpDnControl(switch_input, PUD_UP);
     while (1){
          if(digitalRead(switch_input))
               digitalWrite(LED,LOW);    /* off on GPIO */
          else
               digitalWrite(LED, HIGH);  /* on on GPIO */

          }
     }
```

Interfacing DHT

Figure 3-3 showcases the DHT sensors' GPIO connections.

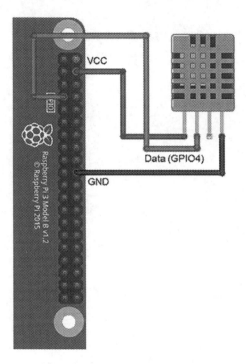

Figure 3-3. *GPIO connections of DHT sensors*

```
sudo python setup.py install
```

Assign the appropriate sensor type to this library's sensor variable. Here, you're going to use a DHT11 sensor.

```
sensor = Adafruit_DHT.DHT11
```

If someone is using the DHT22 sensor, you must assign Adafruit DHT. DHT22 to the sensor variable, as shown in Figure 3-4. Then assign the pin number to which the data pin of the DHT sensor is connected. The DHT11 sensor's output is connected to GPIO4, as illustrated in the preceding interface diagram.

```
import Adafruit_DHT

sensor = Adafruit_DHT.DHT11
pin = 4
while True:
    humidity, temperature = Adafruit_DHT.read_
    retry(sensor, pin)
    print('Temp={0:0.1f}*C  Humidity={1:0.1f}%'.
    format(temperature, humidity))
if humidity is not None and temperature is not None:
    print('Temp={0:0.1f}*C  Humidity={1:0.1f}%'.
    format(temperature, humidity))
else:
    print(Try again!')
```

The output of this program's results are shown in Figure 3-4.

```
                                              *Python 3.4.2 Sh
 File  Edit  Shell  Debug  Options  Windows  Help

>>> ================================= RESTART =
>>>
Temp=26.00*C  Humidity=44.00%
Temp=26.00*C  Humidity=45.00%
Temp=27.00*C  Humidity=43.00%
Temp=27.00*C  Humidity=43.00%
Temp=27.00*C  Humidity=43.00%
Temp=26.00*C  Humidity=44.00%
Temp=26.00*C  Humidity=44.00%
Temp=26.00*C  Humidity=44.00%
Temp=26.00*C  Humidity=44.00%
Temp=26.00*C  Humidity=44.00%
Temp=26.00*C  Humidity=44.00%
Temp=26.00*C  Humidity=44.00%
Temp=26.00*C  Humidity=44.00%
Temp=26.00*C  Humidity=45.00%
Temp=26.00*C  Humidity=45.00%
Temp=26.00*C  Humidity=45.00%
Temp=26.00*C  Humidity=39.00%
Temp=27.00*C  Humidity=43.00%
Temp=27.00*C  Humidity=47.00%
Temp=27.00*C  Humidity=45.00%
Temp=27.00*C  Humidity=47.00%
Temp=27.00*C  Humidity=48.00%
Temp=28.00*C  Humidity=56.00%
Temp=27.00*C  Humidity=53.00%
Temp=27.00*C  Humidity=52.00%
Temp=27.00*C  Humidity=51.00%
Temp=27.00*C  Humidity=51.00%
```

Figure 3-4. DHT sensor output

Interfacing Pi cam to Raspberry Pi zero w

Figure 3-5 shows the RPI JATAG-based sensor.

Figure 3-5. RPI cam

The Pi camera module is a high-definition camera that can capture still images and video in high definition. The Raspberry Pi board features a CSI (camera serial interface) that enables direct connection to the Pi camera module. This Pi camera module connects via a 15-pin ribbon cable to the Raspberry Pi's CSI port.

Pi Camera Specifications

This chapter uses Pi camera version 1.3. The following are its characteristics.

- Resolution: 5 megapixels
- HD Video recording
  - 1080p @30 frames per second
  - 720p @60 frames per second
  - 960p @45 frames per second

It can capture wide, still (motionless) images with a resolution of 2592×1944 pixels via the CSI interface.

Pi Camera Access

Open the configuration file with the following command to enable the camera on the Raspberry Pi.

```
sudo raspi-config
```

Then select the interfacing options, from which you can enable the camera's functionality.

reboot

You can now access the camera on the Raspberry Pi. Now, you can capture images and videos on the Raspberry Pi using the Pi camera.

```
import picamera
from time import sleep
camera = picamera.PiCamera()
camera.resolution = (1024, 768)
camera.brightness = 60
camera.start_preview()
#add text on image
camera.annotate_text = 'Hello folks'
sleep(5)
#store image
camera.capture('image1.jpeg')
camera.stop_preview()
```

Interfacing PIR Sensor

The PIR sensor detects infrared heat radiations. As a result, they are advantageous for detecting moving living objects that emit infrared heat radiations. When a PIR sensor detects motion, its output (in terms of voltage) is high; when there is no motion, it is low (stationary object or no object). PIR sensors are used in a variety of applications, including room light control via human detection, human motion detection for home security, and so on. Figure 3-6 shows the PIR sensor, and Figure 3-7 shows the PIR sensor with an RPI connection.

Figure 3-6. *PIR sensor*

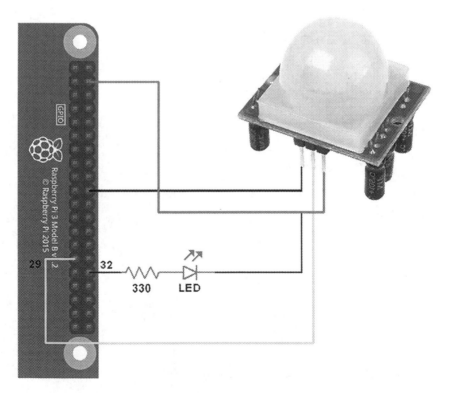

Figure 3-7. *PIR sensor with RPI connection*

```python
import RPi.GPIO as GPIO

PIR_input = 29                          #read signal from pir pin
LED = 32                                #LED for acknowledgement
GPIO.setwarnings(False)
GPIO.setmode(GPIO.BOARD)                #pin configuration
GPIO.setup(PIR_input, GPIO.IN)
GPIO.setup(LED, GPIO.OUT)
GPIO.output(LED, GPIO.LOW)

while True:
#when motion detected turn on LED
    if(GPIO.input(PIR_input)):
        GPIO.output(LED, GPIO.HIGH)
    else:
        GPIO.output(LED, GPIO.LOW)
```

Python

Python is a high-level interpreted programming language. It supports many programming concepts, such as object-oriented and functional programming.

```python
print("Hello, World!")
```

The following shows the output.

```
>>> print("Hello World")
Hello World
```

The following are common Python keywords.

- and: A logical operator

- as: Creates an alias

- break: Breaks out of a loop

- class: Defines a class

- continue: continue to the next iteration of a loop

- def: Defines a function

- del: Deletes an object

- elif: Used in conditional statements, same as else if

- else: Used in conditional statements

- except: Used with exceptions, what to do when an exception occurs

- False: Boolean value, the result of comparison operations

- for: Creates a for loop

- from: Imports specific parts of a module

- global: Declares a global variable

- if: Makes a conditional statement

- import: Imports a module

- in: Checks if a value is present in a list, tuple, etc.

- is: Tests if two variables are equal

- lambda: Creates an anonymous function

- none: Represents a none value

- not: A logical operator

- or: A logical operator

- return: Exits a function and returns a value

- True: Boolean value, the result of comparison operations

- try: Makes a try...except statement

- while: Creates a while loop

File Concepts

The following opens a file.

Syntax: `f = open("demofile.txt", "r")`

The following reads a file.

```
f = open("demofile.txt", "r")
print(f.read())
```

The following shows the output.

```
>>> f=open("C:/              /FILE_OP/demofile.txt","r")
>>> print(f.read())
    Hello! Welcome to demofile.txt
    This File is for testing purpose
    Good Luck!
```

The following reads only parts of a file.

```
f = open("demofile.txt", "r")
print(f.read(5))
```

The following shows the output.

```
>>> f=open("C:/Users/              /demofile.txt","r")
>>> print(f.read(5))
    Hello
>>>
```

The following reads a line.

```
f = open("demofile.txt", "r")
print(f.readline())
```

The following shows the output.

```
>>> f=open("C:/Users/          /demofile.txt","r")
>>> print(f.readline())
    Hello Welcome to demofile.txt
```

The following writes an existing file.

```
f = open("demofile2.txt", "a")
f.write("Now the file has more content!")
f.close()
#open and read the file after the appending:
f = open("demofile2.txt", "r")
print(f.read())
```

The following shows the output.

```
>>> f=open("C:/Users/          /demo.txt","a")
>>> f.write("Now the file has more contents!")
    31
>>> f.close()
>>> f=open("C:/Users/          /demo.txt","r")
>>> print(f.read())
    Hello! welcome to  demefile2.txt
    This file is for testing purpose
    Good luck!

    Now the file has more contents!
>>>
```

The following are the most common file-handling methods.

- close(): Closes the file

- read(): Returns the file content

- readable(): Returns whether the file steam can be read or not

- readline(): Returns one line from the file

- readlines(): Returns a list of lines from the file

- seek(): Change the file position

- seekable(): Returns whether the file allows us to change the file position

- tell(): Returns the current file position

- truncate(): Resizes the file to a specified size

- writable(): Returns whether the file can be written to or not

- write(): Writes the specified string to the file

- writelines(): Writes a list of strings to the file

Spreadsheet Concepts

pandas is used to work on the data. With the help of this module, you can extract data from a database into an Excel spreadsheet, or you can also convert an Excel spreadsheet into a programmatic format. pandas is one of the most popular and favorite data science tools used in Python programming for data wrangling and analysis. And pandas is a game changer in cleaning, transforming, manipulating, and analyzing data.

The following is the code for installing pandas.

```
import pandas as pd
import numpy as np
```

The following is the code for loading and saving data.

```
Pd.readfiletype()      #open a file
df=pd.read_excel('data.xlsx',index_col=0)
df
```

The following shows the output.

```
>>> import pandas as pd
>>> pd.read_excel("C:/Users/           /Desktop/FILE_OP/demo1.xlsx", index_col=0)
            University    Slots
COUNTRY
INDIA         VEL TECH    10000
USA           HARDVARD        4
>>>
```

```
Pd.dataframe()      #convert a certain Python object
(dictionary, lists    etc)
df=pd.dataframe(data=data).t
df
```

The following shows the output.

```
>>> d={'University' :['University of Johannesburg'],'SLOTS':['10000']}
>>> pd.DataFrame(data=d)
                    University    SLOTS
0  University of Johannesburg    10000
```

```
df.to_filetype(filename)  #save a data frame you're working
with/on to different kinds of files (like CSV, Excel, JSON and
SQL tables) df.to_csv('data.csv')
```

The following shows the output.

```
>>> df = pd.DataFrame(data=d)
>>> df.to_csv('C:                            /data.csv')
```

▣ data	23-05-2022 08:13 PM	Microsoft Excel Comma Separated Values File

The following methods are used for viewing and inspecting data.

- df.head(n): Returns the first n rows

- df.tail(n): Returns the last n rows

- df.shape: Returns the number of rows and columns

- df.info: Returns the index, datatype, and memory information

- df.value_counts(dropna=false): Returns unique values and counts for a series (like a column or a few columns)

- df.describe(): Returns summary statistics for numerical column

- df.mean(): Returns the mean of all columns

- df.corr(): Returns the correlation between columns in a data frame

- df.count(): Returns the number of non-null values in each data frame column

- df.max(): Returns the highest value in each column

- df.min(): Returns the lowest value in each column

- df.median(): Returns the median of each column

- df.std(): Returns the standard deviation of each column

The following is used in selecting data.

- (df[col]): Selects a column from the data and returs the data with the col label as an array

- (df[[col1,col2]]): Selects a few columns and returns columns as a new dataframe

- (s.iloc[0]): Selects by position

- (s.loc['index_one']): Selects by index

The following methods are used in filtering, sorting, and grouping data.

- df[df[year]<1987]: Filter columns

- df.sort_values(col1): Column in an ascending order

- df.sort_values(col2,ascending=false): Column in an descending order

- df.sort_values([col1,col2],ascending=[true,false]): Sort values by col1 in ascending order then col2 in descending order

The following methods are used in data cleaning.

- pd.isnull(): Always checks for missing values in the data by running

- pd.isnull()sum. pd.notnull(): Gets a sum of null/missing values

Communication Concepts

Python provides two levels of access to network services. At a low level, you can access the basic socket support in the underlying operating system, allowing you to implement clients and servers for connection-oriented and connectionless protocols.

At a higher level, Python has libraries that provide higher-level access to specific application-level network protocols, such as FTP, HTTP, and so on.

Socket

Sockets are the endpoints of a bidirectional communications channel. Sockets may communicate within a process, between processes on the same machine, or between processes on different continents [3].

Socket Modules

To create a socket, you must use the socket.socket() function available in the socket module, which has the following general syntax. Socket methods are listed and described in Table 3-1.

```
s = socket.socket (socket_family, socket_type, protocol=0)
```

- **socket_family** is either AF_UNIX or AF_INET, as explained earlier.

- **socket_type** is either SOCK_STREAM or SOCK_DGRAM.

- **protocol** is usually left out, defaulting to 0.

Table 3-1. *Socket Methods*

S.no	Method Name	Description
1	s.bind()	Binds addresses to a socket
2	s.listen()	Sets up and starts TCP listener
3	s.accept()	Passively waits/accepts TCP client connection
4	s.connect()	Actively initiates TCP server connection
5	s.recv()	Receives TCP message
6	s.send()	Transmits TCP message
7	s.recvfrom()	Receives UDP message
8	s.sendto()	Transmits UDP message
9	s.close()	Closes socket
10	socket.gethostname()	Returns the hostname

A Simple Server

To write Internet servers, you use the socket function available in the socket module to create a socket object. A socket object is then used to call other functions to set up a socket server. Call the bind(hostname, port) function to specify a port for your service on the given host. Next, call the accept method of the returned object. This method waits until a client connects to the port you specified and then returns a connection object that represents the connection to that client [4].

```python
#!/usr/bin/python          # This is server.py file

import socket              # Import socket module

s = socket.socket()# Create a socket object
host = socket.gethostname()# Get local machine name
```

```
port =12345# Reserve a port for your service.
s.bind((host, port))# Bind to the port

s.listen(5)# Now wait for client connection.
whileTrue:
    c, addr = s.accept()# Establish connection with
    client.print'Got connection from', addr
    c.send('Thank you for connecting')
    c.close()# Close the connection
```

A Simple Client

The socket.connect(hosname, port) opens a TCP connection to the hostname on the port. Once you have a socket open, you can read from it like any IO object. When done, close it.

The following code is a simple client that connects to a given host and port, reads any available data from the socket, and then exits.

```
#!/usr/bin/python          # This is client.py file

import socket              # Import socket module

s = socket.socket()# Create a socket object
host = socket.gethostname()# Get local machine name
port =12345# Reserve a port for your service.

s.connect((host, port))
print s.recv(1024)
s.close()# Close the socket when done
```

The following runs server.py and client.py.

```
$ python server.py &
$ python client.py
```

The following shows the result.

```
@DESKTOP-30T18IP ~\..\file_op >>> py Server.py
Got Connected from  ('127.0.0.1', 64950)
        @DESKTOP-30T18IP ~\..\file_op >>> _
```

```
        @DESKTOP-30T18IP ~\..\file_op >>> py Client.py
Thank you for  b'Connecting'
        @DESKTOP-30T18IP ~\..\file_op >>>
```

Wired and Wireless Programming Concepts

Wireless The following is a sample program.ming Concepts Seeing
a computer without an active Internet connection today is next to
impossible. The Internet has been of the utmost importance in the twenty-
first century. There are multiple ways one can connect their machine to
the Internet. The first is traditional cables (i.e., the Ethernet), and the other
is modern wireless fidelity systems—or Wi-Fi. Wi-Fi has made life easier
and faster for everyone. With a touch of the thumb or a click of the mouse,
you get connected to a limitless ocean of information and resources almost
instantaneously. This section accomplishes the same task with a high-level
modern programming language, like Python.

Connect Wi-Fi Using Python

The following imports the libraries.

```python
import os
```

The following displays all the available SSIDs with the help of cmd
commands and a Python library named os.

```python
os.system('cmd /c "netsh wlan show networks"')
# scan available Wifi networks
```

The following selects a known Wi-Fi to connect to.

```
name_of_router =input('Enter Name/SSID of the Wifi Network you
wish to connect to: ')     # input Wifi name

os.system(f'''cmd /c "netsh wlan connect name={
name_of_router}"''')  # connect to the given wifi network
```

Setting up a New Wi-Fi Network's XML Configuration

The following is the function for the preceding concepts.

```
defcreateNewConnection(name, SSID, password):
    config ="""<?xml version=\"1.0\"?>
<WLANProfile xmlns="http://www.microsoft.com/networking/WLAN/
profile/v1">
    <name>"""+name+"""</name>
    <SSIDConfig>
        <SSID>
            <name>"""+SSID+"""</name>
        </SSID>
    </SSIDConfig>
    <connectionType>ESS</connectionType>
    <connectionMode>auto</connectionMode>
    <MSM>
        <security>
            <authEncryption>
                <authentication>WPA2PSK</authentication>
                <encryption>AES</encryption>
                <useOneX>false</useOneX>
            </authEncryption>
            <sharedKey>
                <keyType>passPhrase</keyType>
                <protected>false</protected>
```

```
        <keyMaterial>"""+password+"""</keyMaterial>
      </sharedKey>
    </security>
  </MSM>
</WLANProfile>"""
    command ="netsh wlan add profile filename=\""+name+".
    xml\""+" interface=Wi-Fi"
    with open(name+".xml", 'w') as file:
        file.write(config)
    os.system(command)

createNewConnection(name, name, password)
# establish new connection
connect(name, name)   # connect to the wifi network
```

Wired Programming Concepts

Python is a useful language thanks to its simplicity, functionality, and platform-independent nature. This section looks at how to use Python with serial ports so you can use it to interact with microcontrollers and other serial-port-enabled devices (including those using virtual ports).

The following code installs PySerial.

```
pip install PySerial  #import the module in python

import serial
```

- The *baud rate* shows how quickly a COM port operates. Arduino projects tend to operate at 115200.

- *The port* is the name of the port being used (find this in the device manager).

- A *parity bit* is used for error correction but are not normally used.

- A *stop bit* signals the end of a frame. Only one is used unless there are timing issues.

- A *time out* prevents the serial port from hanging.

  ```
  serialPort = serial.Serial(port = "COM4",
  baudrate=115200, bytesize=8, timeout=2,
  stopbits=serial.STOPBITS_ONE)
  ```

- open() opens the serial port.

- close() closes the serial port.

- readline() reads a string from the serial port.

- read(size) reads n number of bytes from the serial port.

- write(data) writes the data passed to the function to the serial port.

- in_waiting, a variable, holds the number of bytes in the buffer.

The following opens a port at 9600,8,N,1 with no timeout.

```
>>>ser = serial.Serial('/dev/ttyUSB0')  # open serial port
>>>print(ser.name)          # check which port was really used
>>>ser.write(b'hello')      # write a string
>>>ser.close()              # close port
```

The following opens a port at 38400,8,E,1 with non-blocking HW handshaking.

```
>>>ser=serial.Serial('COM3',38400,timeout=0,parity=serial
.PARITY_EVEN,rtscts=1) # read up to one hundred bytes
>>>s=ser.read(100)# or as much is in the buffer
```

The following configures the ports later.

```
>>>ser=serial.Serial()
>>>ser.baudrate=19200
>>>ser.port='COM1'
>>>ser
Serial<id=0xa81c10, open=False>(port='COM1', baudrate=19200,
bytesize=8, parity='N', stopbits=1, timeout=None, xonxoff=0,
rtscts=0)
>>>ser.open()
>>>ser.is_open
True
>>>ser.close()
>>>ser.is_open
False
```

Node-RED

Node-RED is a programming tool for wiring together hardware devices, APIs, and online services in new and interesting ways. It provides a browser-based editor that makes it easy to wire together flows using a wide range of nodes in the palette that can be deployed to its runtime in a single click [5].

Node-RED Features

- It supports browser-based flow editing.

- As it is built on Node.js, it supports a lightweight runtime environment along with the event-driven and non-blocking model.

- The flows created in Node-RED are stored using JSON, which can be easily imported and exported for sharing with others.

- You can run it locally (Docker support, etc.).

- It can easily fit on most devices, including Raspberry Pi, BeagleBone Black, Arduino, and Android.

- It can run in a cloud environment, such as Bluemix, AWS, and MS Azure.

Node-RED Architecture

- Node-RED (latest version 0.16) is fast because it is driven by the latest supported version of Node.js (LTS 6.x).

- It is an asynchronous io and event-driven architecture.

- It has a single-threaded event queue, which supports simplicity.

- It offers single language support for JavaScript (both from the front end and back end).

- The complete architecture is built using Express, D3, jQuery, and WebSockets.

Node-RED Applications

- In Bluemix, Node-RED is used to connect to IoT (with ReST and MQTT).

- Node-RED is used to bind and connect to databases (e.g., MongoDB).

- Node-RED stores IoT data for present and future computation.

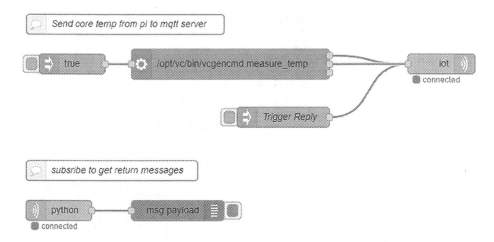

Figure 3-8. *Node-RED implementation*

MQTT Protocols

You could use HiveMQ as an MQQT broker for this explanation. It is a messaging platform for fast, efficient, and reliable data movement to and from connected IoT devices and enterprise systems [6].

The following installs MQQT.

```
pip3 install paho-mqtt (Python 3) / pip install paho-mqtt
(Python 2)
```

The following is sample code.

```
import time
import paho.mqtt.client as paho
from paho import mqtt
def on_connect(client, userdata, flags, rc, properties=None):
    print("Connection received with code %s." % rc)
def on_publish(client, userdata, mid, properties=None):
print("mid: "+str(mid))
```

```python
def on_subscibe(client, userdata, mid, granted_qos,
properties=None):
    print("Subscribed: "+str(mid)+" "+str(granted_qos))
def on_message(client, userdata, msg):
    print(msg.topic+" "+str(msg.qos)+" "+str(msg.payload))
client = paho.Client(client_id="", userdata=None,
protocol=paho.MQTTv5)
client.on_connect = on_connect
client.tls_set(tls_version=mqtt.client.ssl.PROTOCOL_TLS)
client.username_pw_set("username","password") #Use the username
and password of the cluster which you created in hiveMQ server.
client.connect("Broker Server ID", 8883) #Use Server ID of the
cluster allocated.
client.on_subscirbe = on_subscribe
client.on_message = on_message
client.on_publish  = on_publish
client.subscibe("encyclopedia/#", qos=1)
client.publish("encyclopedia/temperature",
payload="hot", qos=1)
client.loop_forever()
```

The following shows the output.

```
Connection received with code Success.
Subscribed: 1 [<paho.mqtt.reasoncodes.ReasonCodes object at 0x000001B9236E0A48>]
encyclopedia/temperature 1 b'hot'
mid: 2
```

Google Sheets Programming (gspread)

gspread is a Python API for Google Sheets.

The following installs gspread.

```
pip install gspread (Python 2) / pip3 install gspread
(Python 3)
```

106

The following is sample code.

```
import gspread
import pandas as pd
from oauth2client.service_account import
ServiceAccountCredentials
# define the scope
scope = ['https://spreadsheets.google.com/feeds','https://www.
googleapis.com/auth/drive']
# add credentials to the account
creds = ServiceAccountCredentials.from_json_keyfile_
name('Script.json', scope) #Use the .json script API downloaded
from google cloud or any other cloud service.
# authorize the clientsheet
client = gspread.authorize(creds)
sheet = client.open('P2S')
sheet_instance = sheet.get_worksheet(0)
record = sheet_instance.get_all_records()
marks = sheet_instance.col_values(3)
print(record)
print(marks)
```

The following shows the output.

```
[{'ID': 1, 'NAME': 'YORU', 'MARKS': 5}, {'ID': 2, 'NAME': 'SAGE', 'MARKS': 3}]
['MARKS', '5', '3']
```

Firebase Programming

Firebase is a platform Google provides to accelerate app development. It offers BaaS or back end as a service, which means that Firebase takes care of cloud infrastructure and all your back-end needs. This lets you develop and deploy faster [7].

The following installs Firebase.

```
pip install firebase_admin (Python 2) / pip3 install firebase_
admin (Python 3)
```

The following is sample code.

```
from firebase import firebase
firebase = firebase.FirebaseApplication("database server
ID",None)
data = {
    'Name':' kanagachidambaresan',
    'Email':' drgrkanagachidambaresan@veltech.edu.in',
    'Phone':9564781254
}
result = firebase.post("/Customer",data)
print(result)
```

The following shows the output.

```
▼ ── Customer
     ▼ ── -N2odQho5nN9-M7_rOZO
              ── Email: "drgrkanagachidambaresan@veltech.edu.in"
              ── Name: "kanagachidambaresan"
              ── Phone: 9564781254
```

Matplotlib

The Matplotlib library for Python is a visualization library for creating many types of graphs, like static graphs, animated graphs, and interactive visualizations. Most Matplotlib utilities lie under the Pyplot submodule and are imported under the plt alias [8].

"import matplotlib.pyplot as plt"

Pyplot is an API for Python's Matplotlib that effectively makes Matplotlib a viable open source alternative. MATLAB is a propriety multi-paradigm programming language and numeric computing environment, which can perform data analysis, graphics, algorithm development, and app building. MATLAB can be used in Python. Pyplot provides Matplotlib with two main features.

- A MATLAB-style interface that allows the users who are familiar with MATLAB to adapt to it easily.

- Statefulness, which Pyplot stores the state of an object when you plot it. This is essential for use in the same loop until plt.close() is encountered in the code.

Matplotlib needs to be installed in the system before everything. It can be installed in many ways. The simplest way is to execute the following code in the command prompt.

"pip3 install matplotlib"

It installs the latest version of Matplotlib, which contains various types of graphs. For example, line graphs, bar graphs, markers, scatter plots, pie charts, polar charts, animations, scales, and 3D plotting.

Matplotlib makes easy things easier and hard things possible. You can create, customize, and extend graphs and do the following.

- Develop quality plots with just a few lines of code.

- Use interactive figures that can zoom and pan

- Take full control of line styles, font properties, axes properties

- Export to several types of file formats.

- Explore tailored functionality provided by third-party packages.

Getting Started

Matplotlib plots the data on figures, the windows that contain one or more axes (an area where points are specified in terms of x,y coordinates). A simple graph is created using the following code.

```
import matplotlib.pyplot as plt
import numpy as np
x = np.array([1,2,3,4,5])
y = np.array([10,15,30,25,50])
plt.plot(x,y)
plt.show()
```

First, the matplotlib.pyplot and NumPy modules need to be imported. NumPy is a module used for matrix operations. Two lists—x points and y points—are created using the NumPy module with values ranging from 0–6 and 0–256. These two list values are then plotted in an empty figure with x points listed as x coordinates and y points as y coordinates. Then plt.show() function is called. This function shows the plotted graph in the figure in a new window. The output graph of the preceding code looks similar to Figure 3-9.

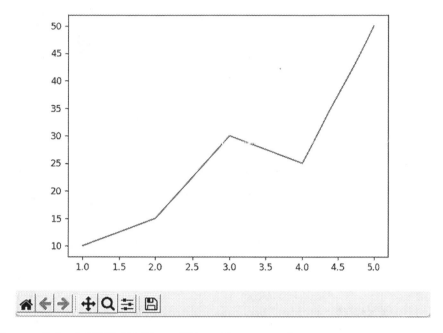

Figure 3-9. *MATLAB Plot of NumPy array elements*

Thus, the simple graph is plotted with some random values of x and y coordinates.

The simplest way of creating a figure with axes is using pyplot.subplots. This pyplot.subplot creates subplots with the required number of axes. Let's create an empty figure using the plt.figure() function, as follows.

```
import matplotlib.pyplot as plt
fig = plt.figure()
plt.show()
```

Figure 3-10 shows the empty figure that is created.

111

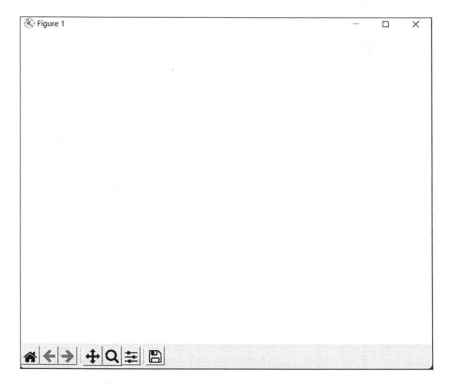

Figure 3-10. *MATLAB plot of an empty figure*

Next, let's add axes to the empty figure.

```
import matplotlib.pyplot as plt
fig = plt.figure()
plt.plot([1,6,8,7])
plt.ylabel('some random numbers')
plt.show()
```

Figure 3-11 shows the output.

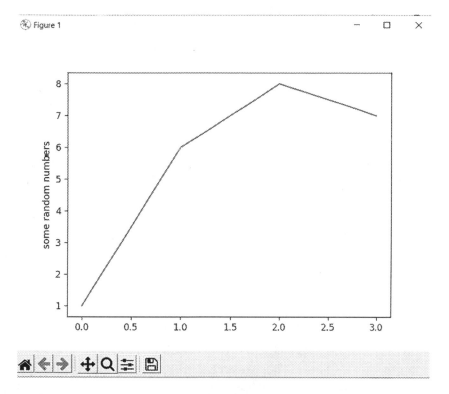

Figure 3-11. *MATLAB plot of random values*

The preceding code used plt.plot() to plot a list of four values. The x axis ranges from 0–3, and the y axis ranges from 1–4. If you provide a list of values to plot, Matplotlib assumes it as a sequence of y values and automatically generates values for x. Since the Python range generally starts at 0, the default value of x axis starts from 0, and it has the same length as y. So, the x values generated are [0,1,2,3]. The plt.ylabel() function sets the label for the y axis. Similarly, plt.xlabel() function for the x axis. The x axis and y axis values limit can also be given so that the output graph can be plotted in a given range. It can be achieved by using plt.xlim() and plt.ylim(). A title can be given to a figure using the plt.title() function.

The following is sample code.

```
Fig = plt.figure()
plt.title("Sample Plot")
plt.plot([1, 3, 3, 4, 8, 9])
plt.ylabel('some numbers')
plt.xlabel("Python Generated Numbers")
plt.xlim(-3,3)
plt.ylim(-4,4)
plt.show()
```

Figure 3-12 shows the output.

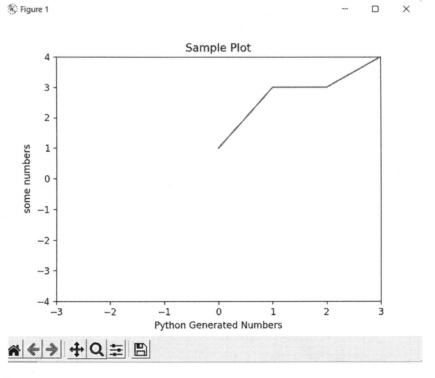

Figure 3-12. *MATLAB plot of Python generated numbers*

This is the output of the preceding code. The x and y axis labels are set. The x axis and y axis ranges are given using xlim(), ylim function. Since the range is negative to positive and the values start at 0, the graph is plotted accordingly.

Multiple Subplots in a Figure

An entire figure can be divided into two or more subplots. Matplotlib makes it easier by using plt.subplot(). Subplots can also be generated using the axes function in Pyplot from Matplotlib.

The following is an example.

```
import numpy as np
import matplotlib.pyplot as plt
x1 = np.linspace(0.0, 5.0)
x2 = np.linspace(0.0, 2.0)
y1 = np.cos(2 * np.pi * x1) * np.exp(-x1)
y2 = np.tan(2 * np.pi * x2)
plt.subplot(2, 1, 1)
plt.plot(x1, y1, 'o-')
plt.title('A tale of 2 subplots')
plt.ylabel('Damped oscillation')
plt.subplot(2, 1, 2)
plt.plot(x2, y2, '.-')
plt.xlabel('time (s)')
plt.ylabel('Undamped')
plt.show()
```

You are going to plot two subplots in a single figure. Four list values are required to plot the graphs. Pyplot gets the values as a list and plots it accordingly. x1, x2, y1, and y2 are the lists created with some values generated using the NumPy array module. Then the plt.subplot(2,1,1).

plt.subplot() has three major parameters: plt.subplot(int,int,int). plt. subplot(1,1,1) is the default. The three integers are (nrows, ncols, index). The subplot takes the index position on a grid with nrows rows and ncols columns. The index starts at 1 in the upper left corner and increases to the right.

subplot(2,1,1) defines two rows, which means two separate plots up and down are plotted separately with the same single column. It has a common figure title and different y labels.

Figure 3-13 shows the output.

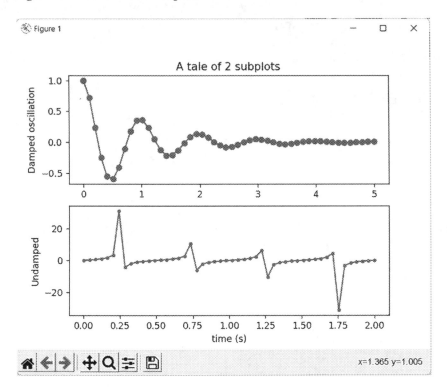

Figure 3-13. *MATLAB plot of tale of two subplots*

Alternative Method for Creating Multiple Plots

Subplots can also be generated by defining the two axes separately.

The following is an example.

```
import numpy as np
import matplotlib.pyplot as plt
x1 = np.linspace(0.0, 5.0)
x2 = np.linspace(0.0, 2.0)
y1 = np.cos(2 * np.pi * x1) * np.exp(-x1)
y2 = np.tan(2 * np.pi * x2)
fig, (ax1, ax2) = plt.subplots(2, 1)
fig.suptitle('A tale of 2 subplots')
ax1.plot(x1, y1, 'o-')
ax1.set_ylabel('Damped oscillation')
ax2.plot(x2, y2, '.-')
ax2.set_xlabel('time (s)')
ax2.set_ylabel('Undamped')
plt.show()
```

The output is the same as the previous method; however, plt. subplot, a Pyplot built-in function, created multiple subplots. Also, an empty figure was created. Two axes—ax1 and ax2—were created using plt.subplots. The plotting of these was done separately. Then, other actions, like setting the label and axes limits—were done. Finally, the graph is shown using plt.show().

Bar Graphs

Bar graphs are best used when showing comparisons between categories. Typically, the bars are proportional to the values they represent and can be plotted either horizontally or vertically. One axis of the chart shows the specific categories being compared, and the other axis represents discrete values.

A bar graph presents categorical data with rectangular bars. Each bar's height or length is proportional to the value it represents. In Python, Matplotlib allows you to create three types of bar graphs: grouped, stacked, and horizontal.

Grouped Bar Graphs

Grouped bar charts compare multiple data items with a single color denoting a specific series across all sets. As with basic bar charts, vertical and horizontal versions of grouped bar charts are available.

Let's look at an example of a vertical grouped bar graph.

```
import matplotlib.pyplot as plt
import numpy as np
labels = ['G1', 'G2', 'G3', 'G4', 'G5']
men_means = [20, 34, 30, 35, 27]
women_means = [25, 32, 34, 20, 25]
x = np.arange(len(labels))  # the label locations
width = 0.35  # the width of the bars
fig, ax = plt.subplots()
rects1 = ax.bar(x - width/2, men_means, width, label='Men')
rects2 = ax.bar(x + width/2, women_means, width, label='Women')
# Add some text for labels, title and custom x-axis tick
labels, etc.
ax.set_ylabel('Scores')
ax.set_title('Scores by group and gender')
ax.set_xticks(x)
ax.set_xticklabels(labels)
ax.legend()
ax.bar_label(rects1, padding=3)
ax.bar_label(rects2, padding=3)
fig.tight_layout()
plt.show()
```

The required modules are imported like every other program. A grouped bar graph compares two or more elements. Here the comparison made is between men_means and women_means list. An empty figure is created using subplots with an x axis. Since you are comparing two lists here, rects1 and rects2 are the variables that are going to represent the data in the men_means and women_means list in the graph. After plotting the data, the axes and the figure should be presented professionally. So, x and y axis labels and limits are mentioned. Figure 3-14 is MATLAB plot grouped bar graph with a legend. The legend identifies the visual elements used to distinguish different groups of data on the graph. The legend helps you evaluate the effects of grouping.

Figure 3-14 shows the output.

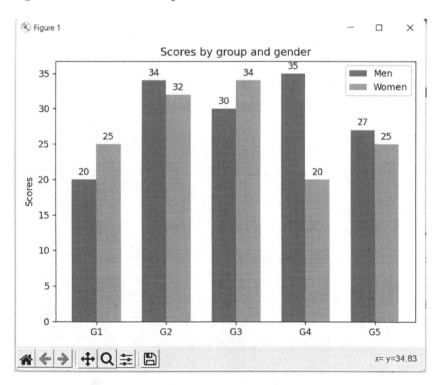

Figure 3-14. *MATLAB plot of grouped bar graph*

Stacked Bar Graphs

A stacked bar graph is a graph that uses bars to show comparisons
between categories of data but with the ability to break down and compare
parts of a whole. Each bar in the chart represents a whole, and segments in
the bar represent different parts or categories of that whole.

The following is an example.

```python
import matplotlib.pyplot as plt
labels = ['G1', 'G2', 'G3', 'G4', 'G5']
men_means = [25, 30, 34, 22, 20]
women_means = [30, 34, 31, 23, 25]
width = 0.35        # the width of the bars: can also be len(x)
                    sequence
fig, ax = plt.subplots()
ax.bar(labels, men_means, width, label='Men')
ax.bar(labels, women_means, width,  bottom=men_means,
label='Women')
ax.set_ylabel('Scores')
ax.set_title('Scores by group and gender')
ax.legend()
y_offset = -15
for bar in ax.patches:
    ax.text(
        # Put the text in the middle of each bar. get_x returns
          the start
        # so we add half the width to get to the middle.
          bar.get_x() + bar.get_width() / 2,
        # Vertically, add the height of the bar to the start of
          the bar,
        # along with the offset.
          bar.get_height() + bar.get_y() + y_offset,
```

```
    # This is actual value we'll show.
      round(bar.get_height()),
    # Center the labels and style them a bit.
      ha='center',
    color='w',
    weight='bold',
    size=8
  )
plt.show()
```

The stacked bar graphs compare two or more categories or values and represent them in a single bar with different colors to identify each category. Here the men_means and women_means are the two lists that will be compared. The program is similar to the grouped bar graph, including only one change in the ax.bar function. The first ax.bar represents the men_means list; the second represents the women_means list, where "bottom" is mentioned. Bottom is a keyword and a parameter to the ax.bar function wherein the compared categories, which category should be at the bottom of the stack. In the bar, men_means is at the bottom, and women_means is at the top. A "for" looping statement marks the values of the corresponding bar and category inside its corresponding stack.

Figure 3-15 shows the output.

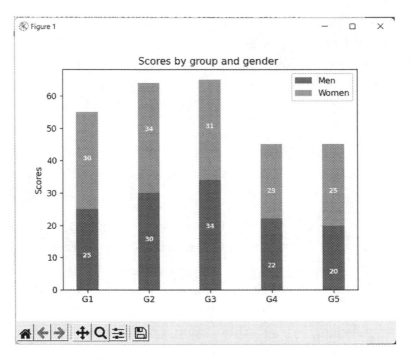

Figure 3-15. *MATLAB plot of stacked bar graph*

Horizontal Bar Graph

In this type, the variables or the data categories have to be written. The rectangular bars are horizontally drawn on the y axis, and the x axis shows the length of the bars equal to the values of different variables present in the data.

The following is an example.

```python
import matplotlib.pyplot as plt
import numpy as np
fig, ax = plt.subplots()
# Example data
people = ('Tom', 'Jerry', 'Doraemon', 'ShinChan', 'Pokemon')
y_pos = np.arange(len(people))
```

```
performance = 3 + 10 * np.random.rand(len(people))
ax.barh(y_pos, performance, align='center')
ax.set_yticks(y_pos)
ax.set_yticklabels(people)
ax.invert_yaxis()  # labels read top-to-bottom
ax.set_xlabel('Performance')
ax.set title('How fast do you want to go today?')
plt.show()
```

The implementation of the horizontal bar graph is simple. The figure and axes are created. For the y axis, a list of five people is considered; for the x axis, values are generated randomly and stored in a "performance" list. Usually, ax.bar() represents a bar graph. But in this case, ax.barh() plots the values in the y axis. The bars are positioned at y with the given alignment. The horizontal baseline is left (default 0). Then plt.show() represents the plotted graph.

Figure 3-16 shows the output.

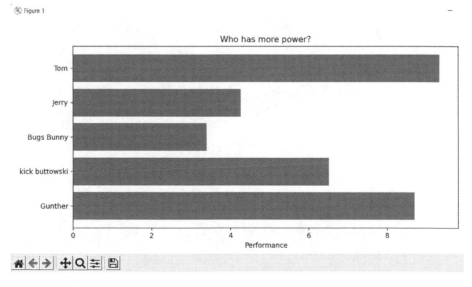

Figure 3-16. *MATLAB plot of horizontal bar graph*

Scatter Plot

A scatter plot is a type of plot or mathematical diagram using Cartesian coordinates to display values for typically two variables for a set of data. Scatter plots are primarily used to observe and show relationships between two numeric variables. The dots in a scatter plot report the values of individual data points and patterns when the data are taken as a whole.

The following is an example.

```
import matplotlib.pyplot as plt
x = [3,5,7,7,12,7,22,19,4,1,2,9,16]
y = [89,76,97,78,101,96,113,67,64,48,87,80,81]
plt.scatter(x, y)
plt.ylabel('Y')
plt.xlabel("X")
plt.title("Scatter Plot")
plt.show()
```

Two lists of equal length with some values are considered. It is plotted using plt.scatter(list1,list2), which plots the values of x and y in the corresponding coordinates. The label and title are given, and the graph is shown using plt.show().

Figure 3-17 shows the output.

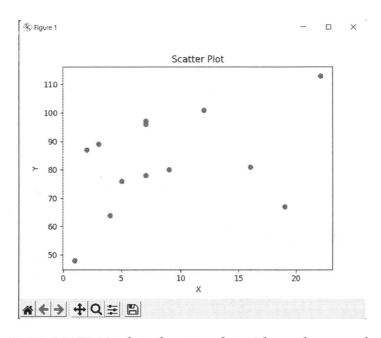

Figure 3-17. *MATLAB plot of scatter plot with random numbers*

Scatter Custom Symbol

Creating a scatter plot with a custom symbol. Many different types of symbols can be used to plot the graph. A custom ellipse symbol is used to plot in the scatter plot.

The following is an example.

```
import matplotlib.pyplot as plt
import numpy as np
# unit area ellipse
rx, ry = 6., 3.
area = rx * ry * np.pi
theta = np.arange(0, 2 * np.pi + 0.01, 0.1)
verts = np.column_stack([rx / area * np.cos(theta), ry / area *
np.sin(theta)])
x,  s = np.random.rand(2, 30)
```

125

```
s *= 10**2.
fig, ax = plt.subplots()
ax.scatter(x, s, marker=verts)
plt.show()
```

The area of the ellipse is fixed to mark in the graph. A verts variable is defined, where the measurements about the ellipse is stored, which is then mentioned in the ax.scatter()as marker=verts. Then two lists—x and s— with random values are generated and are marked in the figure.

Figure 3-18 shows the output.

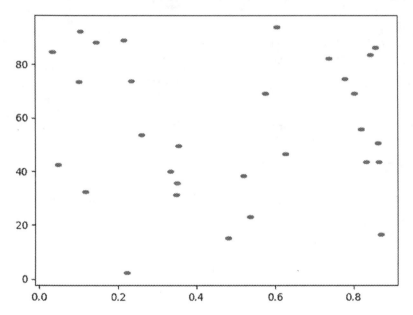

Figure 3-18. *MATLAB plot of scatter plot with custom symbol*

Spectrum Representation

Matplotlib can also be used for spectrum representations. A signal is a function of time that is represented by a series of sinusoidal components. These sinusoidal components have different amplitudes, frequencies, phases, and magnitudes. Thus, the plotting of the frequency versus the sinusoidal components' amplitude and phase comprise a signal called a *frequency spectrum* or the spectrum of a signal. The frequency spectrum of a discrete-time signal is calculated using a *fast Fourier transform* (FFT).

A Fourier analysis of a periodic function refers to the extraction of a series of sines and cosines. This analysis is called a *Fourier series*. FFT is a mathematical method for transforming a function of time into a function of frequency. It is very useful for time-dependent phenomena. The resulting spectrum shows the frequency component of the given input signal [9].

The following is an example.

```
import matplotlib.pyplot as plt
import numpy as np
np.random.seed(0)
dt = 0.01  # sampling interval
Fs = 1 / dt  # sampling frequency
t = np.arange(0, 10, dt)
# generate noise:
nse = np.random.randn(len(t))
r = np.exp(-t / 0.05)
cnse = np.convolve(nse, r) * dt
cnse = cnse[:len(t)]
s = 0.1 * np.sin(4 * np.pi * t) + cnse  # the signal
fig, axs = plt.subplots(nrows=3, ncols=2, figsize=(7, 7))
# plot time signal:
axs[0, 0].set_title("Signal")
axs[0, 0].plot(t, s, color='b')
axs[0, 0].set_xlabel("Time")
axs[0, 0].set_ylabel("Amplitude")
# plot different spectrum types:
```

```
axs[1, 0].set_title("Magnitude Spectrum")
axs[1, 0].magnitude_spectrum(s, Fs=Fs, color='r')
axs[1, 1].set_title("Log. Magnitude Spectrum")
axs[1, 1].magnitude_spectrum(s, Fs=Fs, scale='dB', color='k')
axs[2, 0].set_title("Phase Spectrum ")
axs[2, 0].phase_spectrum(s, Fs=Fs, color='m')
axs[2, 1].set_title("Angle Spectrum")
axs[2, 1].angle_spectrum(s, Fs=Fs, color='c')
axs[0, 1].remove()  # don't display empty ax
fig.tight_layout()
plt.show()
```

Figure 3-19 shows the output.

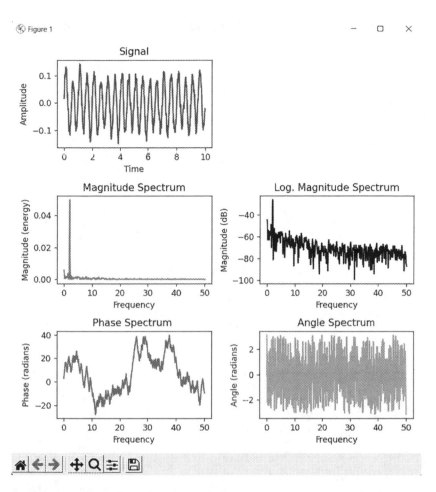

Figure 3-19. *The plots show the different spectrum graphs for a sine signal*

Coherence of Two Signals

In signal processing, coherence is the statistic value used to examine the relationship between the two signals or data. Coherent signals are signals that have the same phase and frequency. The coherence function measures the correlation between two signals as a function of their frequency components. It is thus a correlation spectrum.

The following example shows how to plot the coherence of two signals using Python Matplotlib.

```python
import numpy as np
import matplotlib.pyplot as plt
# Fixing random state for reproducibility
np.random.seed(19680801)

dt = 0.01
t = np.arange(0, 30, dt)
nse1 = np.random.randn(len(t))                    # white noise 1
nse2 = np.random.randn(len(t))                    # white noise 2

# Two signals with a coherent part at 10Hz and a random part
s1 = np.sin(2 * np.pi * 10 * t) + nse1
s2 = np.tan(2 * np.pi * 10 * t) + nse2

fig, axs = plt.subplots(2, 1)
axs[0].plot(t, s1, t, s2)
axs[0].set_xlim(0, 2)
axs[0].set_xlabel('time')
axs[0].set_ylabel('s1 and s2')
axs[0].set_title('Two signals S1 and S2')
axs[0].grid(True)

cxy, f = axs[1].cohere(s1, s2, 256, 1. / dt)
axs[1].set_ylabel('coherence')

fig.tight_layout()
plt.show()
```

Random values are obtained and formed as an array using the NumPy module. Two signals with a coherent part at 10 Hz and a random part are created and are named s1 and s2. Then an empty figure is created with two axes subplots. Then, the axes find coherence between the signals s1 and s2.cohere function in Matplotlib.

The axes.cohere() function in the axes module of the Matplotlib library plots the coherence between two signals, x and y.

Coherence is the normalized cross-spectral density.

$$C_{xy} = \frac{|P_{xy}|^2}{P_{xx}P_{yy}}$$

Figure 3-20 shows the output.

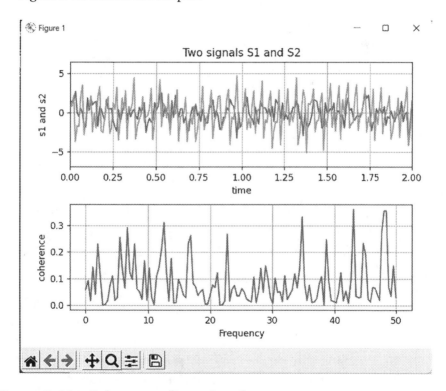

Figure 3-20. *Coherence of two signals*

Cross-Correlation Graph

Cross-correlation is a measurement that tracks the movements of two or more sets of time series data relative to one another. It compares multiple time series and determines how well they match up with each other and at what point the best match occurs. It is also known as a *sliding-dot product* or *sliding-inner product*. The time series data's correlation coefficient range is from –1 to +1. The closer the cross-correlation value is to 1, the more likely the sets are identical.

The following is an example.

```
import matplotlib.pyplot as plt
import numpy as np

# Fixing random state for reproducibility
np.random.seed(196)

x, y = np.random.randn(2, 100)
fig, ax1 = plt.subplots()
ax1.xcorr(x, y, usevlines=True, maxlags=25, normed=True, lw=2)
ax1.set_title("Cross-Correlation")
ax1.set_xlabel("X values")
ax1.set_ylabel("Y values")
ax1.grid(True)

plt.show()
```

As usual, two sample lists with random values are created. The figure and axes are formed. Then the values of the two lists are plotted in a special manner using ax1.xcorr(). The Axes.xcorr() function plots the correlation between x and y. Finally, the labels and titles are mentioned and shown using plt.show().

Figure 3-21 shows the output.

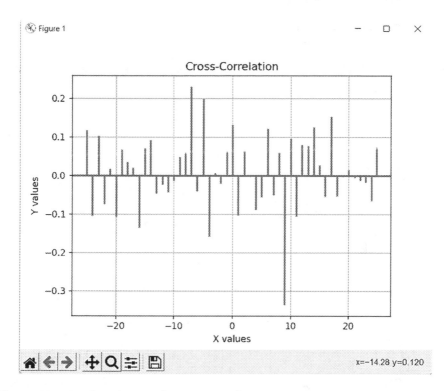

Figure 3-21. *Cross-correlation graph*

Autocorreleation Graph

Autocorrelation is a mathematical representation of the degree of similarity between a given time series and a lagged version of itself over successive time intervals. Autocorrelation, sometimes known as *serial correlation* in the discrete-time case, is the correlation of a signal with a delayed copy of itself as a delay function.

The following is an example.

```python
import matplotlib.pyplot as plt
import numpy as np
# Fixing random state for reproducibility
np.random.seed(200)
```

133

```
x, y = np.random.randn(2, 100)
fig, ax1 = plt.subplots()
ax1.acorr(x, usevlines=True, normed=True, maxlags=25, lw=2)
ax1.set_title("Auto-Correlation")
ax1.set_xlabel("X values")
ax1.set_ylabel("Y values")
ax1.grid(True)
plt.show()
```

Figure 3-22 shows the output.

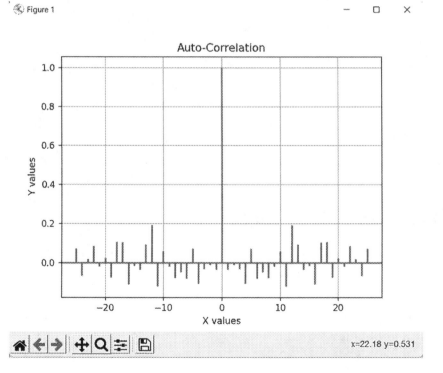

Figure 3-22. *Autocorrelation graph*

Changing Figure Size in Different Units

The figure size of a figure can be changed or set to a particular value using the plt.figure(figsize=(x,y)) function, where x, y is the size measurements given in inches, which is the default. The figure size can be given in the following units.

- Inches (default)

- Centimeters

- Pixels

Multiplying centimeter-based numbers with a conversion factor from cm to inches gives the right numbers. Naming the conversion factor cm makes the conversion almost look like appending a unit to the number, which is nicely readable. Similarly, one can use conversion from pixels.

The following is an example.

```
import matplotlib.pyplot as plt
text_kwargs = dict(ha='center', va='center', fontsize=28,
color='m')
plt.subplots(figsize=(6, 2))
plt.text(0.5, 0.5, '6 inches x 2 inches', **text_kwargs)
cm = 1/2.54  # centimeters in inches
plt.subplots(figsize=(15*cm, 5*cm))
plt.text(0.5, 0.5, '15cm x 5cm', **text_kwargs)
px = 1/plt.rcParams['figure.dpi']  # pixel in inches
plt.subplots(figsize=(600*px, 200*px))
plt.text(0.5, 0.5, '600px x 200px', **text_kwargs)
plt.show()
```

Figure 3-23 shows the output.

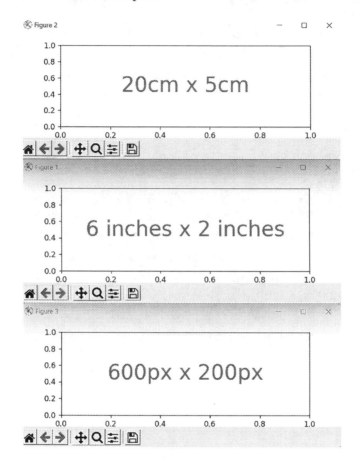

Figure 3-23. *Changing figure size in different units*

Scale

Two plots on the same axes with different left and right scales. The trick is using two axes that share the same x axis. You can use separate matplotlib.ticker formatters and locators as desired since the two axes are independent. Such axes are generated by calling the Axes.twinx method. Likewise, Axes.twiny is available to generate axes that share a y axis but have different top and bottom scales.

The following is an example.

```
import numpy as np
import matplotlib.pyplot as plt

# Create some mock data
t = np.arange(0.01, 10.0, 0.01)
data1 = np.exp(t)
data2 = np.cos(2 * np.pi * t)

fig, ax1 = plt.subplots()

plt.title("Plots with different scale")
color = 'tab:red'
ax1.set_xlabel('time (s)')
ax1.set_ylabel('exp', color=color)
ax1.plot(t, data1, color=color)
ax1.tick_params(axis='y', labelcolor=color)

ax2 = ax1.twinx()  # instantiate a second axes that shares the
same x-axis

color = 'tab:blue'
ax2.set_ylabel('sin', color=color)  # we already handled the
x-label with ax1
ax2.plot(t, data2, color=color)
ax2.tick_params(axis='y', labelcolor=color)

fig.tight_layout()  # otherwise the right y-label is
slightly clipped
plt.show()
```

Two data lists are created using np.array. Then two subplots are created, and the data lists are plotted in the same figure, identifying the two graphs in different colors. The tight layout is then shown as a graph using plt.show().

Figure 3-24 shows the output.

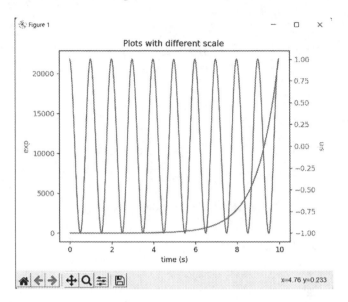

Figure 3-24. *Plots with different scale*

Pie Charts

A pie chart is a circular statistical graphic divided into slices to illustrate numerical proportions. In a pie chart, the arc length of each slice is proportional to the quantity it represents. While it is named for its resemblance to a pie that has been sliced, there are variations in how it can be presented.

Pie charts are widely used in the business world and mass media. They have been criticized, and many experts recommend avoiding them as research has shown it is difficult to compare different sections of a given pie chart or data across different pie charts. Pie charts can be replaced in most cases by other plots, such as bar charts, box plots, and dot plots.

The Matplotib API has a pie() function that generates a pie diagram representing data in an array. The fractional area of each wedge is given by x/sum(x).

If sum(x) < 1, then the values of x are given the fractional area directly, and the array is not normalized.

The following is a sample program.

```
import matplotlib.pyplot as plt
# Pie chart, where the slices will be plotted
counter-clockwise:
labels = 'Chemistry', 'Social', 'Maths', 'Physics'
sizes = [10, 35, 43, 12]
explode = (0, 0.1, 0, 0)  # only "explode" the 2nd slice
(i.e. 'Hogs')
fig1, ax1 = plt.subplots()
ax1.pie(sizes, explode=explode, labels=labels,
autopct='%1.1f%%', shadow=True, startangle=90)
ax1.axis('equal')  # Equal aspect ratio ensures that pie is
drawn as a circle.
plt.show()
```

Figure 3-25 shows the output.

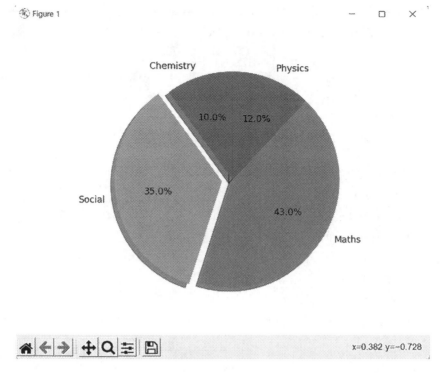

Figure 3-25. *MATLAB plot of pie chart*

Nested Pie Charts

In this case, pie takes values corresponding to counts in a group. First, let's generate some fake data corresponding to three groups. In the inner circle, treat each number as belonging to its own group. In the outer circle, plot them as members of their original three groups.

The following is a sample program.

```python
import matplotlib.pyplot as plt
import numpy as np
fig, ax = plt.subplots()
size = 0.3
vals = np.array([[55., 37.], [32., 45.], [24., 15.]])
```

```
cmap = plt.get_cmap("tab20c")
outer_colors = cmap(np.arange(3)*4)
inner_colors = cmap([1, 2, 5, 6, 9, 10])
ax.pie(vals.sum(axis=1), radius=1, colors=outer_colors,
wedgeprops=dict(width=size, edgecolor='w'))
ax.pie(vals.flatten(), radius=1-size, colors=inner_colors,
wedgeprops=dict(width=size, edgecolor='w'))
ax.set(aspect="equal", title='Pie plot with `ax.pie`')
plt.show()
```

Figure 3-26 shows the output.

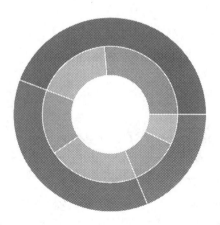

Figure 3-26. *MATLAB plot of pie chart*

141

Labeling a Pie and a Donut

A donut chart is a variant of a pie chart. There is a hole in its center and it displays categories as arcs rather than slices. Both charts make part-to-whole relationships easy to understand at a glance. First, you define the imports and create a figure with subplots.

Starting with a pie chart, let's create the data and a list of labels from it.

Provide a function to the auto pct argument, which expands automatic percentage labeling by showing absolute values. Calculate the latter from relative data and the known sum of all values.

The following is a program for labeling a pie chart.

```python
import numpy as np
import matplotlib.pyplot as plt
fig, ax = plt.subplots(figsize=(6, 3),
subplot_kw=dict(aspect="equal"))
recipe = ["200 g Ice-cream",
          "80 g sugar",
          "100 g Cheese",
          "250 g milk",
          "100 g water"]
data = [float(x.split()[0]) for x in recipe]
ingredients = [x.split()[-1] for x in recipe]
def func(pct, allvals):
    absolute = int(round(pct/100.*np.sum(allvals)))
    return "{:.1f}%\n({:d} g)".format(pct, absolute)
wedges, texts, autotexts = ax.pie(data, autopct=lambda pct:
func(pct, data), textprops=dict(color="w"))
ax.legend(wedges, ingredients,
          title="Ingredients",
          loc="center left",
          bbox_to_anchor=(1, 0, 0.5, 1))
```

```
plt.setp(autotexts, size=8, weight="bold")
ax.set_title("Matplotlib bakery: A pie")
plt.show()
```

Figure 3-27 shows the output.

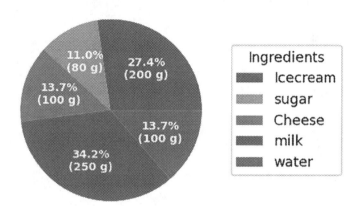

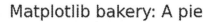

Figure 3-27. *MATLAB plot of pie chart (bakery)*

The following is a program for labeling a donut chart.

```
import numpy as np
import matplotlib.pyplot as plt
fig, ax = plt.subplots(figsize=(6, 3),
subplot_kw=dict(aspect="equal"))
recipe = ["200 g flour", "80 g sugar", "100 g butter",
"250 g milk", "100 g berries"]
```

```
data = [float(x.split()[0]) for x in recipe]
ingredients = [x.split()[-1] for x in recipe]
def func(pct, allvals):
    absolute = int(round(pct/100.*np.sum(allvals)))
    return "{:.1f}%\n({:d} g)".format(pct, absolute)
wedges, texts, autotexts = ax.pie(data, autopct=lambda pct:
func(pct, data), textprops=dict(color="w"))
ax.legend(wedges, ingredients,
          title="Ingredients",
          loc="center left",
          bbox_to_anchor=(1, 0, 0.5, 1))
plt.setp(autotexts, size=8, weight="bold")
ax.set_title("Matplotlib bakery: A pie")
plt.show()
```

Figure 3-28 shows the output.

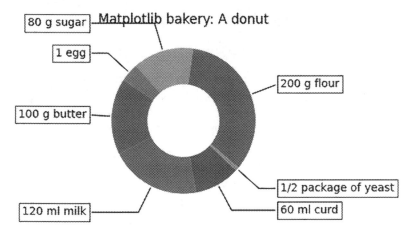

Figure 3-28. *MATLAB plot of donut pie chart*

Style Sheets

A web style sheet is a form of separation of presentation and content for web design in which the markup of a webpage contains the page's semantic content and structure but does not define its visual layout. There are many types of style sheets, and two of those are explained from the style sheets.

FiveThirtyEight Style Sheet

FiveThirtyEight, sometimes rendered as 538, is an American website focusing on opinion poll analysis, politics, economics, and sports blogging.

The following is a sample program.

```
import matplotlib.pyplot as plt
import numpy as np
plt.style.use('fivethirtyeight')
x = np.linspace(0, 10)
np.random.seed(240)
fig, ax = plt.subplots()
ax.plot(x, np.sin(x) + x + np.random.randn(50))
ax.plot(x, np.sin(x) + 8.0 * x + np.random.randn(50))
ax.plot(x, np.sin(x) + 4 * x + np.random.randn(50))
ax.plot(x, np.sin(x) - 8.0 * x + np.random.randn(50))
ax.plot(x, np.sin(x) - 4 * x + np.random.randn(50))
ax.plot(x, np.sin(x) + np.random.randn(50))
ax.set_title("'fivethirtyeight' style sheet")
plt.show()
```

Figure 3-29 shows the output.

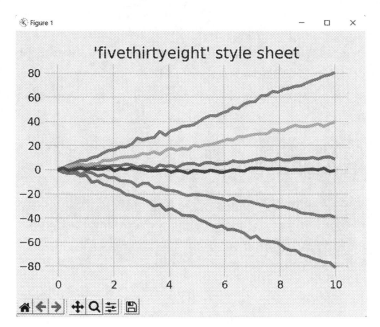

Figure 3-29. *MATLAB plot of FiveThirtyEight style sheet*

Solarized Light Style Sheet

A solarized light style sheet is another graph for plotting values with random lines.

The following is a sample program.

```
import matplotlib.pyplot as plt
import numpy as np
np.random.seed(420)
x = np.linspace(0, 10)
with plt.style.context('Solarize_Light2'):
    plt.plot(x, np.sin(x) + x + np.random.randn(50))
    plt.plot(x, np.sin(x) + 2 * x + np.random.randn(50))
```

```
plt.plot(x, np.sin(x) + 3 * x + np.random.randn(50))
plt.plot(x, np.sin(x) + 4 + np.random.randn(50))
plt.plot(x, np.sin(x) + 5 * x + np.random.randn(50))
plt.plot(x, np.sin(x) + 6 * x + np.random.randn(50))
plt.plot(x, np.sin(x) + 7 * x + np.random.randn(50))
plt.plot(x, np.sin(x) + 8 * x + np.random.randn(50))
# Number of accent colors in the color scheme
plt.title('8 Random Lines - Line')
plt.xlabel('x label', fontsize=14)
plt.ylabel('y label', fontsize=14)
plt.show()
```

Figure 3-30 shows the output.

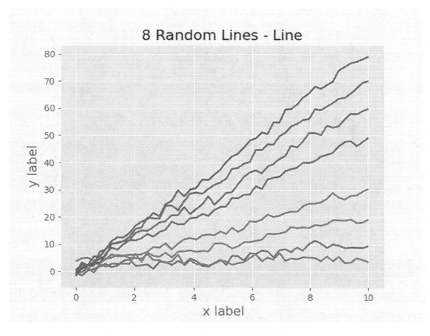

Figure 3-30. *MATLAB plot of Solarized Light style sheet*

3D Graphs

A *three-dimensional space* is a geometric setting in which three values are required to determine the position of an element. This is the informal meaning of the term *dimension*. In geometry, a three-dimensional shape can be defined as a solid figure, object, or shape with three dimensions: length, width, and height.

Plotting 2D Data on a 3D Plot

The following is a sample program.

```
import numpy as np
import matplotlib.pyplot as plt

ax = plt.figure().add_subplot(projection='3d')
# Plot a sin curve using the x and y axes.
x = np.linspace(0, 1, 100)
y = np.cos(x * 2 * np.pi) / 2 + 0.5
ax.plot(x, y, zs=0, zdir='z', label='curve in (x, y)')
# Plot scatterplot data (20 2D points per colour) on the x
and z axes.
colors = ('r', 'm', 'c', 'k')
# Fixing random state for reproducibility
np.random.seed(240)
x = np.random.sample(20 * len(colors))
y = np.random.sample(20 * len(colors))
c_list = []
for c in colors:
    c_list.extend([c] * 20)
```

```
# By using zdir='y', the y value of these points is fixed to
the zs value 0
# and the (x, y) points are plotted on the x and z axes.
ax.scatter(x, y, zs=0, zdir='y', c=c_list, label='points in
(x, z)')
# Make legend, set axes limits and labels
ax.legend()
ax.set_xlim(0, 1)
ax.set_ylim(0, 1)
ax.set_zlim(0, 1)
ax.set_xlabel('X')
ax.set_ylabel('Y')
ax.set_zlabel('Z')
# Customize the view angle so it's easier to see that the
scatter points lie
# on the plane y=0
ax.view_init(elev=20., azim=-35)
plt.show()
```

Figure 3-31 shows the output.

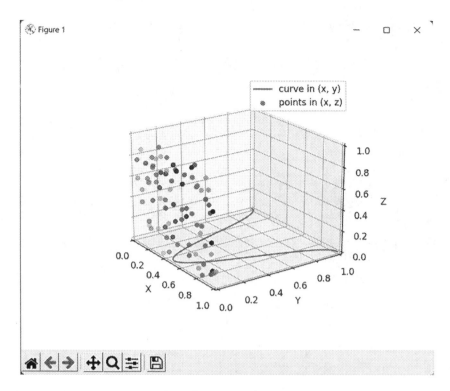

Figure 3-31. *MATLAB plot of 3D graphs*

Creating 2D Bar Graphs in Different Planes

The following is a sample program.

```
import matplotlib.pyplot as plt
import numpy as np

# Fixing random state for reproducibility
np.random.seed(240)
fig = plt.figure()
ax = fig.add_subplot(projection='3d')
colors = ['r', 'm', 'c', 'y']
yticks = [3, 2, 1, 0]
```

```
for c, k in zip(colors, yticks):
    # Generate the random data for the y=k 'layer'.
    xs = np.arange(20)
    ys = np.random.rand(20)
    # You can provide either a single color or an array with
        the same length as
    # xs and ys. To demonstrate this, we color the first bar of
        each set cyan.
    cs = [c] * len(xs)
    cs[0] = 'c'
    # Plot the bar graph given by xs and ys on the plane y=k
        with 80% opacity.
    ax.bar(xs, ys, zs=k, zdir='y', color=cs, alpha=0.8)
ax.set_xlabel('X')
ax.set_ylabel('Y')
ax.set_zlabel('Z')
# On the y axis let's only label the discrete values that we
have data for.
ax.set_yticks(yticks)
plt.show()
```

Figure 3-32 shows the output.

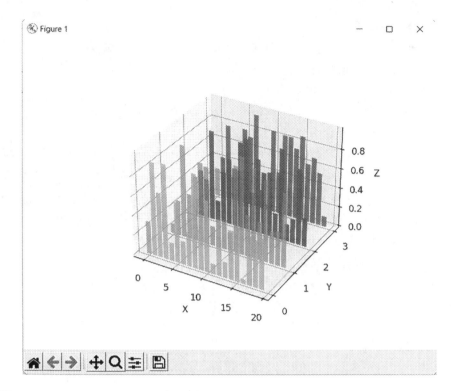

Figure 3-32. *MATLAB plot of 2D graphs*

Creating a 3D Histogram of 2D Data

The following is a sample program.

```
import matplotlib.pyplot as plt
import numpy as np

# Fixing random state for reproducibility
np.random.seed(240)
fig = plt.figure()
ax = fig.add_subplot(projection='3d')
x, y = np.random.rand(2, 100) * 5
hist, xedges, yedges = np.histogram2d(x, y, bins=4,
range=[[0, 4], [0, 4]])
```

```
# Construct arrays for the anchor positions of the 16
bars.xpos, ypos = np.meshgrid(xedges[:-1] + 0.25, yedges[:-1]
+ 0.25, indexing="ij")
xpos = xpos.ravel()
ypos = ypos.ravel()
zpos = 0
# Construct arrays with the dimensions for the 16 bars.
dx = dy = 0.5 * np.ones_like(zpos)
dz = hist.ravel()
ax.bar3d(xpos, ypos, zpos, dx, dy, dz, zsort='average')
plt.show()
```

Figure 3-33 shows the output.

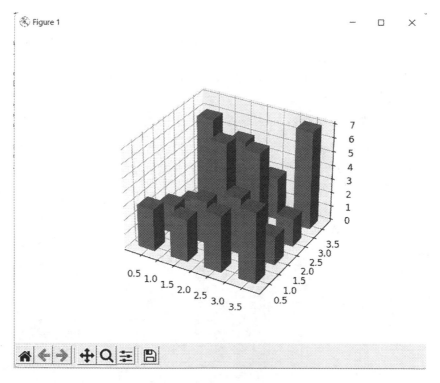

Figure 3-33. *MATLAB plot of 3D histogram of 2D data*

3D Surfaces

The following is a sample program.

```python
import matplotlib.pyplot as plt
from matplotlib import cm
from matplotlib.ticker import LinearLocator
import numpy as np

fig, ax = plt.subplots(subplot_kw={"projection": "3d"})
# Make data.
X = np.arange(-5, 5, 0.25)
Y = np.arange(-5, 5, 0.25)
X, Y = np.meshgrid(X, Y)
R = np.sqrt(X**2 + Y**2)
Z = np.cos(R)
# Plot the surface.
surf = ax.plot_surface(X, Y, Z, cmap=cm.coolwarm, linewidth=0,
antialiased=False)
# Customize the z axis.
ax.set_zlim(-1.01, 1.01)
ax.zaxis.set_major_locator(LinearLocator(10))
# A StrMethodFormatter is used automatically
ax.zaxis.set_major_formatter('{x:.02f}')
# Add a color bar which maps values to colors.
fig.colorbar(surf, shrink=0.5, aspect=5)
plt.show()
```

Figure 3-34 shows the output.

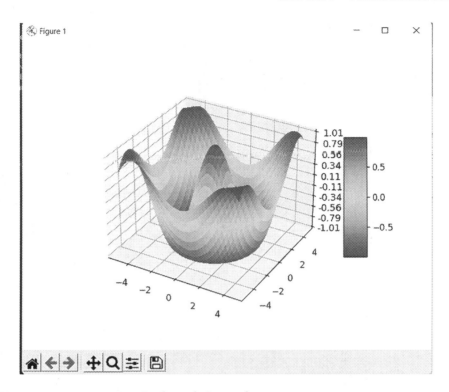

Figure 3-34. *MATLAB plot of 3D surface*

Animation

Matplotlib has a very special animation function. The easiest way to make a live animation in Matplotlib is to use the Animation classes.

Live Line Graph

In this Matplotlib Animation function, an example of how to create live updating graphs that can update their plots live as the data-source updates. You may want to use this for graphing real-time stock prices, or maybe you have a sensor connected to your computer, and you want to display the live sensor data. To do this, you use the animation functionality with Matplotlib.

155

The following is an example.

```python
import matplotlib.pyplot as plt
import matplotlib.animation as animation
from matplotlib import style
style.use('fivethirtyeight')
fig = plt.figure()
ax1 = fig.add_subplot(1,1,1)
def animate(i):
    graph_data = open('example.txt','r').read()
    lines = graph_data.split('\n')
    xs = []
    ys = []
    for line in lines:
        if len(line) > 1:
            x, y = line.split(',')
            xs.append(float(x))
            ys.append(float(y))
    ax1.clear()
    ax1.plot(xs, ys)
ani = animation.FuncAnimation(fig, animate, interval=1000)
plt.show()
```

Here, the only new import is the matplotlib.animation as animation. This is the module that allows you to animate the figure. In the animate function, you build the data and then plot it in the figure. A notepad file named example.txt contains the following data.

[(1,6),(2,3),(3,4),(4,7),(5,2),(6,9),(7,5),(8,9),(9,1),(10,3)]

This data is stored in the notepad and updated in real time. The graph plots its point accordingly.

This is the function of the animate function from Matplotlib.

Figure 3-35 shows the output.

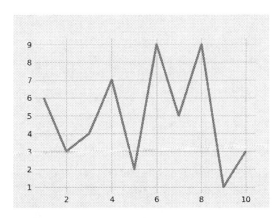

Figure 3-35. *MATLAB plot of live line graph*

The values get updated from the example.txt file and the graph moves on according to the x axis.

Oscilloscope Live

Oscilloscopes test and display voltage signals as waveforms, which are visual representations of voltage variation over time. The signals are plotted on a graph showing how the signal changes. The vertical (y) access represents the voltage measurement, and the horizontal (x) axis represents time. One of the biggest advantages of oscilloscopes is that they give real-time analysis. This means you get the right reading once you connect the device to a power source. This oscilloscope graph can be implemented using Matplotlib [10].

The following is an implementation.

```
import numpy as np
from matplotlib.lines import Line2D
import matplotlib.pyplot as plt
import matplotlib.animation as animation
from IPython import display
```

```python
class Scope:
    def __init__(self, ax, maxt=2, dt=0.02):
        self.ax = ax
        self.dt = dt
        self.maxt = maxt
        self.tdata = [0]
        self.ydata = [0]
        self.line = Line2D(self.tdata, self.ydata)
        self.ax.add_line(self.line)
        self.ax.set_ylim(-.1, 1.1)
        self.ax.set_xlim(0, self.maxt)
        self.ax.set_xlabel("Time in secs")
        self.ax.set_ylabel("Voltage")
        self.ax.set_title("Live Oscilloscope")

    def update(self, y):
        lastt = self.tdata[-1]
        if lastt > self.tdata[0] + self.maxt:  # reset
        the arrays
            self.tdata = [self.tdata[-1]]
            self.ydata = [self.ydata[-1]]
            self.ax.set_xlim(self.tdata[0], self.tdata[0] +
            self.maxt)

            self.ax.figure.canvas.draw()

        t = self.tdata[-1] + self.dt
        self.tdata.append(t)
        self.ydata.append(y)
        self.line.set_data(self.tdata, self.ydata)
        return self.line,
```

```
def emitter(p=0.1):
    """Return a random value in [0, 1) with probability p,
    else 0."""
    while True:
        v = np.random.rand(1)
        if v > p:
            yield 0.
        else:
            yield np.random.rand(1)

# Fixing random state for reproducibility
np.random.seed(240 // 10)

fig, ax = plt.subplots()
scope = Scope(ax)

# pass a generator in "emitter" to produce data for the
update func
ani = animation.FuncAnimation(fig, scope.update, emitter,
interval=50, blit=True)
plt.show()
```

The entire program is divided into two parts: the main and the class, which has a few subfunctions defined within it.

There are two functions inside the Scope class: __init__ and update. The __init__ function is the main function, in which the subplot is created, and the x,y limits and labels are defined.

The update function plays a major role in animation. It plots graphs accordingly with the incoming values generated by the emitter function.

Figure 3-36 shows the output.

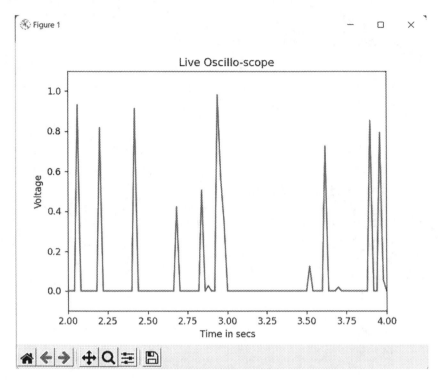

Figure 3-36. *MATLAB plot of oscilloscope live graph*

The values are updated in the plot, and since the x axis limit is set to a particular value, the axis is updated accordingly.

Thus, with the help of the Matplotlib library from Python, many types of graphs have been created and explained. Matplotlib is a Python plotting package that makes it simple to create two-dimensional and three-dimensional plots from data stored in various data structures, including lists, NumPy arrays, and pandas dataframes. matplotlib.pyplot is a collection of functions that make Matplotlib work like MATLAB. Each Pyplot function changes a figure (e.g., creates a figure, creates a plotting area in a figure, plots some lines in a plotting area, decorates the plot with labels, etc.).

References

[1] N. K. Sabat, U. C. Pati, B. R. Senapati, and S. K. Das, "An IoT Concept for Region Based Human Detection Using PIR Sensors and FRED Cloud," 2019 IEEE 1st International Conference on Energy, Systems and Information Processing (ICESIP), 2019, pp. 1–4, doi: 10.1109/ICESIP46348.2019.8938286.

[2] Gabriel Gaspar, Peter Fabo, Michal Kuba, Juraj Ďuďák, and Eduard Nemlaha, MicroPython as a Development Platform for IoT Applications, 2020, doi: 10.1007/978-3-030-51965-0_34.

[3] Socket – Low-level networking interface, `https://docs.python.org/3/library/socket.html`

[4] Network basics, `https://docs.micropython.org/en/latest/esp8266/tutorial/network_basics.html`

[5] G. R. Kanagachidambaresan, "Node-Red Programming and Page GUI Builder for Industry 4.0 Dashboard Design," Springer, Cham, Role of Single Board Computers (SBCs) in rapid IoT Prototyping, 2021, pp. 121–140.

[6] Biswajeeban Mishra and Attila Kertesz, The Use of MQTT in M2M and IoT Systems: A Survey, IEEE Access, Volume 8, 2020.

[7] L. Goswami and P. Agrawal, "IOT based Diagnosing of Fault Detection in Power Line Transmission through GOOGLE Firebase database," 2020 4th International Conference on Trends in Electronics and Informatics (ICOEI) (48184), 2020, pp. 415–420, doi: 10.1109/ICOEI48184.2020.9143007.

[8] Matplotlib, `https://matplotlib.org/`

[9] Spectrum Representations, `https://matplotlib.org/stable/gallery/lines_bars_and_markers/spectrum_demo.html`

[10] W. Cai, B. Wang, and S. Zhang, "Remote Control and Data Acquisition of Multiple Oscilloscopes Using LabVIEW," 2019 International Conference on Smart Grid and Electrical Automation (ICSGEA), 2019, pp. 136–140, doi: 10.1109/ICSGEA.2019.00039.

CHAPTER 4

Wireless Connectivity in IoT

Introduction

The Internet of Things (IoT) starts with connecting to and gathering information on nearby devices. The connectivity is attained wired and wirelessly. The vast and multidimensional devices follow a star, mesh, and hybrid topology with popular IoT wireless technologies. These connections each have advantages and disadvantages. They can be tailored through IoT user cases. Figure 4-1 compares the cost of wireless technologies.

© G. R. Kanagachidambaresan 2022
G. R. Kanagachidambaresan, *Internet of Things Using Single Board Computers*,
https://doi.org/10.1007/978-1-4842-8108-6_4

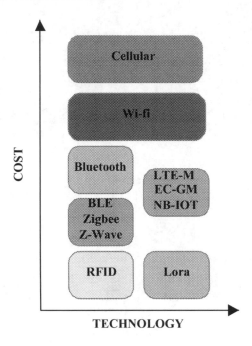

Figure 4-1. *Tech-cost comparison of wireless*

This chapter explains these wireless technologies and how to program them through Arduino and other single-board computers [8].

Low-Power Wide-Area Networks (LPWANs)

In the Internet of Things, low-power wide-area networks (LPWANs) [1] are fairly new. This group of technologies supports large-scale IoT networks that span huge industrial and business campuses. They allow long-range communication on small, cheap batteries that last for years. LPWANs can connect to almost any kind of IoT sensor. They can be used for many applications, such as tracking assets, monitoring the environment, managing a building, detecting occupancy, and keeping track of consumables. On the other hand, LPWANs can only send small blocks of data at a slow rate. This makes them better for applications that don't need a lot of bandwidth or need to be done quickly.

LPWANs aren't all made equal. Today, there are licensed (NB-IoT, LTE-M) and unlicensed (MYTHINGS, LoRa, Sigfox, etc.) technologies, and each one performs differently in key network factors. For example, licensed cellular based LPWANs care most about how much power they use, whereas unlicensed alternatives care more about the quality of service and scalability. Standardization is another consideration if you want to ensure long-term stability, security, and interoperability.

Let's discuss what makes this group of wireless IoT technologies important. The LoRa [2] tech stack is shown in Figure 4-2.

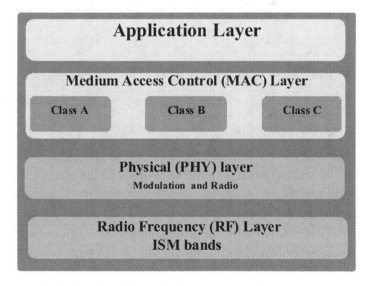

Figure 4-2. *LoRa tech protocol stack*

Figures 4-3 and 4-4 showcase the circuit connection of the LoRa sender with the Arduino UNO and the LoRa receiver with the Arduino Nano.

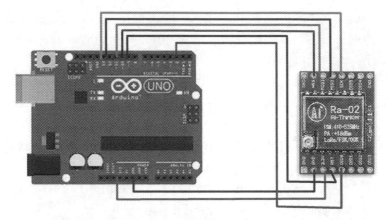

Figure 4-3. *Arduino connected with LoRa radio sender*

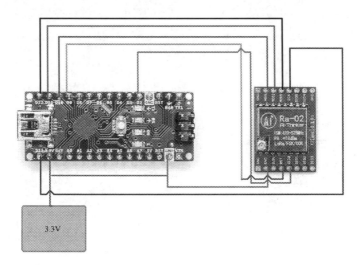

Figure 4-4. *LoRa received connected with Arduino Nano*

```
#include <SPI.h>
#include <LoRa.h>
int counter = 0;

void setup() {
  Serial.begin(9600);
  while (!Serial);
```

```
  Serial.println("LoRa Sender");
  if (!LoRa.begin(433E6)) {
    Serial.println("Starting LoRa failed!");
    while (1);
  }
  LoRa.setTxPower(20);

}

void loop() {
  Serial.print("Sending packet: ");
  Serial.println(counter);

  // send packet
  LoRa.beginPacket();
  LoRa.print("hello ");
  LoRa.print(counter);
  LoRa.endPacket();

  counter++;

  delay(5000);
}
```

//receiver code

```
#include <SPI.h>
#include <LoRa.h>

void setup() {
  Serial.begin(9600);
  while (!Serial);

  Serial.println("LoRa Receiver");
```

```
  if (!LoRa.begin(433E6)) {
    Serial.println("Starting LoRa failed!");
    while (1);
  }
}

void loop() {
  // try to parse packet
  int packetSize = LoRa.parsePacket();
  if (packetSize) {
    // received a packet
    Serial.print("Received packet '");

    // read packet
    while (LoRa.available()) {
      Serial.print((char)LoRa.read());
    }

    // print RSSI of packet
    Serial.print("' with RSSI ");
    Serial.println(LoRa.packetRssi());
  }
}
```

RFID Protocol

Passive RFID [3] tags are different from most other digital radio systems because they have limitations. Because the tags are cheap and don't have much intelligence, they can't use advanced modulations like phase-shift keying or quadrature-amplitude modulation (QAM). Also, turning off the power from the reader reduces the power available to the tag, so the best modulations for the reader are those in which the power is on most of the time. However, these modulations are not good at using the spectrum, so they result in channels that are wide or data rates that are slow. The phase or amplitude of the tag reflection can be changed. However, the small tag reflection is added to large antenna reflections and reflections from the environment, so the signal at the reader may change when the phase or amplitude of the tag reflection changes. You can only hope to notice changes in the antenna's state, not its nature. You can count the number of edges in the tag but can't determine the absolute or differential phase or amplitude. These rules must be considered when choosing tag and reader symbols. Figure 4-5 shows how RFIDs are set up and the bands they use to talk.

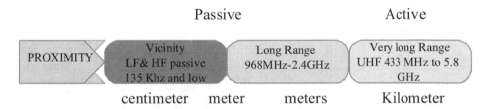

Figure 4-5. *RFID configs and communication bands*

This chapter mainly discusses the Arduino-based programming of passive tags for ID verification purposes. Figure 4-6 illustrates the Arduino and passive RFID connection through the SPI communication protocol [9]. Figure 4-6 demonstrates the RFID connection with Arduino UNO.

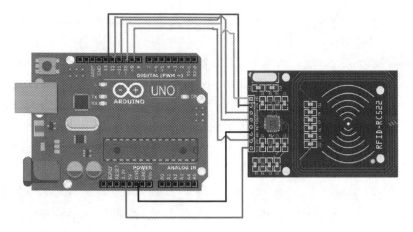

Figure 4-6. *RFID connection with Arduino*

Arduino Code

```
#include <SPI.h>
#include <MFRC522.h>
constexpr uint8_t RST_PIN = 9;      // Configurable, see typical
                                       pin layout above
constexpr uint8_t SS_PIN = 10;      // Configurable, see typical
                                       pin layout above
MFRC522 rfid(SS_PIN, RST_PIN); // Instance of the class
MFRC522::MIFARE_Key key;

// Init array that will store new NUID
byte nuidPICC[4];

void setup() {
  Serial.begin(9600);
  SPI.begin(); // Init SPI bus
  rfid.PCD_Init(); // Init MFRC522
```

```
  for (byte i = 0; i < 6; i++) {
    key.keyByte[i] = 0xFF;
  }

  Serial.println(F("This code scan the MIFARE Classsic
  NUID."));
  Serial.print(F("Using the following key:"));
  printHex(key.keyByte, MFRC522::MF_KEY_SIZE);
}

void loop() {

  // Look for new cards
  if ( ! rfid.PICC_IsNewCardPresent())
    return;

  // Verify if the NUID has been readed
  if ( ! rfid.PICC_ReadCardSerial())
    return;

  Serial.print(F("PICC type: "));
  MFRC522::PICC_Type piccType = rfid.PICC_GetType(rfid.
  uid.sak);
  Serial.println(rfid.PICC_GetTypeName(piccType));

  // Check is the PICC of Classic MIFARE type
  if (piccType != MFRC522::PICC_TYPE_MIFARE_MINI &&
    piccType != MFRC522::PICC_TYPE_MIFARE_1K &&
    piccType != MFRC522::PICC_TYPE_MIFARE_4K) {
    Serial.println(F("Your tag is not of type MIFARE
    Classic."));
    return;
  }
```

```
  if (rfid.uid.uidByte[0] != nuidPICC[0] ||
    rfid.uid.uidByte[1] != nuidPICC[1] ||
    rfid.uid.uidByte[2] != nuidPICC[2] ||
    rfid.uid.uidByte[3] != nuidPICC[3] ) {
    Serial.println(F("A new card has been detected."));

    // Store NUID into nuidPICC array
    for (byte i = 0; i < 4; i++) {
      nuidPICC[i] = rfid.uid.uidByte[i];
    }

    Serial.println(F("The NUID tag is:"));
    Serial.print(F("In hex: "));
    printHex(rfid.uid.uidByte, rfid.uid.size);
    Serial.println();
    Serial.print(F("In dec: "));
    printDec(rfid.uid.uidByte, rfid.uid.size);
    Serial.println();
  }
  else Serial.println(F("Card read previously."));

  // Halt PICC
  rfid.PICC_HaltA();

  // Stop encryption on PCD
  rfid.PCD_StopCrypto1();
}

void printHex(byte *buffer, byte bufferSize) {
  for (byte i = 0; i < bufferSize; i++) {
    Serial.print(buffer[i] < 0x10 ? " 0" : " ");
    Serial.print(buffer[i], HEX);
  }
}
```

```
/**
 * Helper routine to dump a byte array as dec values to Serial.
 */
void printDec(byte *buffer, byte bufferSize) {
  for (byte i = 0; i < bufferSize; i++) {
    Serial.print(buffer[i] < 0x10 ? " 0" : " ");
    Serial.print(buffer[i], DEC);
  }
}
```

The data from the passive tag can be seen in the serial monitor after executing this code.

XBEE Radios with Arduino

Zigbee [4] is a long-range wireless protocol that can work in AT and API (application programming interface) modes. The transparent mode (AT) mode is mainly used to transmit one-to-one data. However, the API mode shares GPIO signals and API commands. Figure 4-7 illustrates the basic Zigbee protocol stack.

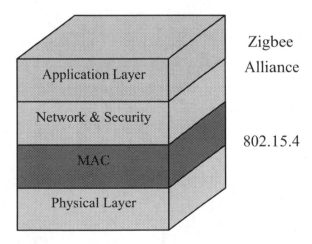

Figure 4-7. *Zigbee protocol basic stack*

Figure 4-8 is a connection diagram of Arduino UNO with an XBee radio.

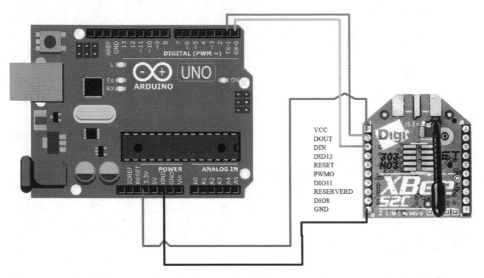

Figure 4-8. *XBee radio connected with serial data transfer with XBee radio*

```
//Configuration

Code //
int led = 13;
int received = 0;
int i;
void setup() {
  Serial.begin(9600);
  pinMode(led, OUTPUT);
}

void loop() {
  if (Serial.available() > 0) {
received = Serial.read();
```

```
if (received == 'a'){
digitalWrite(led, HIGH);
delay(2000);
digitalWrite(led, LOW);
}
 else if (received == 'b'){
   for(i=0;i<5;i++){
digitalWrite(led, HIGH);
delay(1000);
digitalWrite(led, LOW);
delay(1000);
}
}
}
}
```

Once the code is executed on both the sender and receiver sides, a blinking LED can be observed on the receiver side.

Bluetooth with Arduino

Bluetooth [5] is a WPAN technology mainly used for low-range communication like text, voice, and in rare cases, video data. Bluetooth is mainly used for low-distance fast communications. Figure 4-9 illustrates the Bluetooth protocol stack.

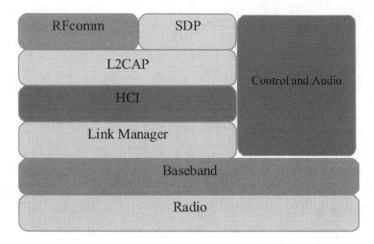

Figure 4-9. *Bluetooth protocol stack*

Figure 4-10 illustrates the HC-05 connected to Arduino through serial ports RX and TX.

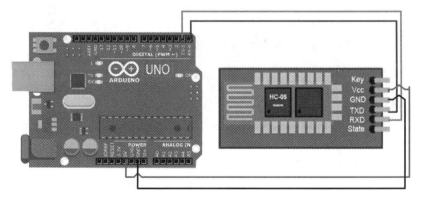

Figure 4-10. *HC-05 connection with Arduino serial communication*

```
char inputByte;
void setup() {
 Serial.begin(9600);
 pinMode(13,OUTPUT);

}
```

```
void loop() {
while(Serial.available()>0){
  inputByte= Serial.read();
  Serial.println(inputByte);
  if (inputByte=='Z'){
  digitalWrite(13,HIGH);
  }
  else if (inputByte=='z'){
  digitalWrite(13,LOW);
  }
  }
}
```

Arduino with a GSM Modem

GSM architecture is a layered model that allows two systems to communicate. The lower layers guarantee the upper-layer protocols' services. Each layer sends appropriate notifications to ensure that the data is correctly prepared, transferred, and received. Figure 4-11 showcases the Arduino connection with the GSM and GPS modules [6]. The GPS location gathered is messaged to a particular programmed number through the GSM service. The Arduino code to perform this follows Figure 4-11.

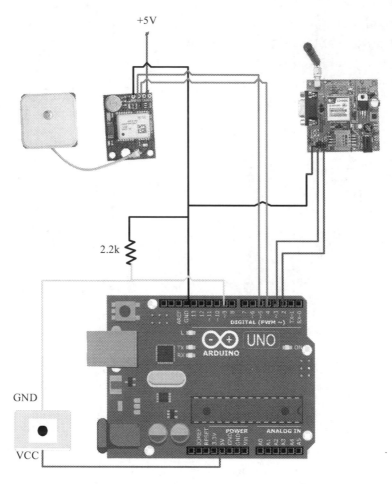

Figure 4-11. *Arduino connection with GSM and GPS module*

Code for interfacing arduino with GPS and GSM sensors.

```
//Sharing GPS information with the user
#include <SoftwareSerial.h>
#include <TinyGPS.h>

int state = 0;
const int pin = 9;
float gpslat, gpslon;
```

```
TinyGPS gps;
SoftwareSerial sgps(4, 5);
SoftwareSerial sgsm(2, 3);

void setup()
{
  sgsm.begin(9600);
  sgps.begin(9600);
}

void loop()
{
sgps.listen();
  while (sgps.available())
  {
    int c = sgps.read();
    if (gps.encode(c))
    {
      gps.f_get_position(&gpslat, &gpslon);
    }
  }
    if (digitalRead(pin) == HIGH && state == 0) {
      sgsm.listen();
      sgsm.print("\r");
      delay(1000);
      sgsm.print("AT+CMGF=1\r");
      delay(1000);
      /*Replace XXXXXXXXXX to 10 digit mobile number &
        ZZ to 2 digit country code*/
      sgsm.print("AT+CMGS=\"+ZZXXXXXXXXXX\"\r");
      delay(1000);
```

```
    //The text of the message to be sent.
    sgsm.print("Latitude :");
    sgsm.println(gpslat, 6);
    sgsm.print("Longitude:");
    sgsm.println(gpslon, 6);
    delay(1000);
    sgsm.write(0x1A);
    delay(1000);
    state = 1;
  }
if (digitalRead(pin) == LOW) {
    state = 0;
  }
    delay(100);
}
```

Arduino with Firebase Cloud Connectivity

This section explains how to program NodeMCU to connect to Google Firebase [7]. Figure 4-12 shows the Anonymous enable feature in Google Cloud Platform (GCP).

- Create an ESP8266 Firebase Project and store data in the Firebase Realtime Database.

- Read data from the Firebase Realtime Database with an ESP8266.

First, perform the following steps.

1. Go to Firebase. Use a Google account to sign in.

2. Click Get Started and Add Project to start a new project.

3. Name your project (e.g., ESP demo).

4. Set the authentication and enable anonymous data handling.

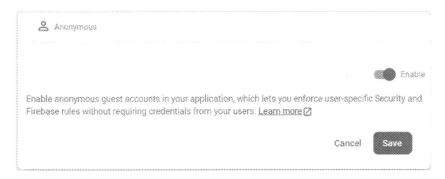

Figure. 4-12. *Anonymous enabled in Google Firebase*

Next, create a Firebase Realtime Database and start in test mode. Set the read and write permissions to true. Copy the Web API key from the Firebase project's settings. Figure 4-13 showcases the NodeMCU connection with Firebase.

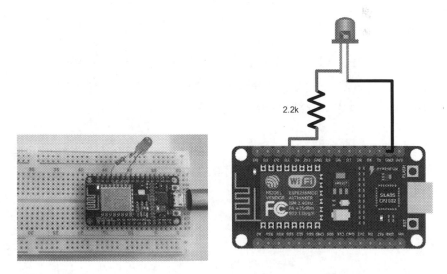

Figure 4-13. *NodeMCU connection with led controlled via Google Firebase*

Figure 4-14. *Firebase Realtime Database showing LEDSTATUS*

The following code snippet helps NodeMCU switch the LED on and off.

```
//Arduino code

#include <ESP8266WiFi.h>
                                                // esp8266 library
#include <FirebaseArduino.h>
                                                // firebase library
#define FIREBASE_HOST "your-project.firebaseio.com"
                            // the project name address from
                                 firebase id
#define FIREBASE_AUTH "06dEpqanFg**************qAwnQLwLI"
                        // the secret key generated from firebase
#define WIFI_SSID "xxxxxxxxxxxxx"
                                                // input your home or
                                                   public wifi name
#define WIFI_PASSWORD "xxxxxxxxxxxxxx"
                                          //password of wifi ssid

String fireStatus = "";
                                          // led status received from
                                             firebase
```

```
int led = D3;                          // for external led
void setup() {
  Serial.begin(9600);
  delay(1000);
  pinMode(LED_BUILTIN, OUTPUT);
  pinMode(led, OUTPUT);
  WiFi.begin(WIFI_SSID, WIFI_PASSWORD);
                          // try to connect with wifi
  Serial.print("Connecting to ");
  Serial.print(WIFI_SSID);
  while (WiFi.status() != WL_CONNECTED) {
    Serial.print(".");
    delay(500);
  }
  Serial.println();
  Serial.print("Connected to ");
  Serial.println(WIFI_SSID);
  Serial.print("IP Address is : ");
  Serial.println(WiFi.localIP());
                          //print local IP address
  Firebase.begin(FIREBASE_HOST, FIREBASE_AUTH);
                                  // connect to firebase
  Firebase.setString("LED_STATUS", "OFF");
                                  // send initial string of
                                  led status
}

void loop() {
  fireStatus = Firebase.getString("LED_STATUS");
                                  // get ld status input
                                  from firebase
```

```
  if (fireStatus == "ON") {
                                    // compare the input of led
                                       status received from firebase
    Serial.println("Led Turned ON");
    digitalWrite(LED_BUILTIN, LOW);
                                    // make bultin led ON
    digitalWrite(led, HIGH);
                      // make external led ON
  }
  else if (fireStatus == "OFF")
{                                  // compare the input of led
                                       status received from firebase
    Serial.println("Led Turned OFF");
    digitalWrite(LED_BUILTIN, HIGH);
                                    // make bultin led OFF
    digitalWrite(led, LOW);
                                    // make external led OFF
  }
  else {
    Serial.println("Wrong Credential! Please send ON/OFF");
  }
}
```

References

[1] Q. M. Qadir, T. A. Rashid, N. K. Al-Salihi, B. Ismael, A. A. Kist, and Z. Zhang, "Low Power Wide Area Networks: A Survey of Enabling Technologies, Applications and Interoperability Needs," *IEEE Access*, vol. 6, 2018, pp. 77454–77473. doi: 10.1109/ACCESS.2018.2883151.

[2] U. Noreen, A. Bounceur, and L. Clavier, "A study of LoRa low power and wide area network technology," 2017 International Conference on

Advanced Technologies for Signal and Image Processing (ATSIP), 2017, pp. 1–6. doi: 10.1109/ATSIP.2017.8075570.

[3] R. Rayhana, G. Xiao, and Z. Liu, "RFID Sensing Technologies for Smart Agriculture," *IEEE Instrumentation & Measurement Magazine*, vol. 24, no. 3, May 2021, pp. 50–60. doi: 10.1109/MIM.2021.9436094.

[4] S. Long, F. Miao, "Research on ZigBee wireless communication technology and its application," 2019 IEEE 4th Advanced Information Technology, Electronic and Automation Control Conference (IAEAC), 2019, pp. 1830–1834. doi: 10.1109/IAEAC47372.2019.8997928.

[5] P. Priya, V. V. Prabhu, and S. Saravanan, "Improving the Performance Efficiency of Village Pond Cleaner Using Arduino in the Basis of Bluetooth Controlled Process," 2021 Second International Conference on Electronics and Sustainable Communication Systems (ICESC), 2021, pp. 971–974. doi: 10.1109/ICESC51422.2021.9532762.

[6] Ma May Thet Htar and Ma Hnin Yu Myaing, "GSM Based Home Automation System Using Arduino," *International Journal of Trend in Scientific Research and Development* (IJTSRD), vol. 3, no. 5, August 2019, pp. 1666–1669. https://doi.org/10.31142/ijtsrd26806

[7] Wu-Jeng Li, Chiaming Yen, You-Sheng Lin, Shu-Chu Tung, and Shih-Miao Huang, "JustIoT Internet of Things based on the Firebase Real-time Database," IEEE, 2018. doi: 10.1109/SMILE.2018.8353979.

[8] Jonathan Álvarez Ariza and Heyson Baez, "Understanding the role of single-board computers in engineering and computer science education: A systematic literature review," *Computer Applications in Engineering Education*, 2021.

[9] Dawoud Shenouda Dawoud and Peter Dawoud, "6 Serial Peripheral Interface (SPI)," *Serial Communication Protocols and Standards RS232/485, UART/USART, SPI, USB, INSTEON, Wi-Fi and WiMAX*, River Publishers, 2020, pp. 191–244.

## CHAPTER 5

The Internet of Things Through the Raspberry Pi

Introduction

Raspberry Pi is an elegant, low-cost single-board computer mainly used for rapid prototyping and building small IoT applications [1]. Together with sensors and other communication modules, it can play an important role in making decisions in a smart environment. Figure 5-1 showcases the different Raspberry Pi configurations, communication modules, and available ports.

G. R. Kanagachidambaresan, *Internet of Things Using Single Board Computers*,
https://doi.org/10.1007/978-1-4842-8108-6_5

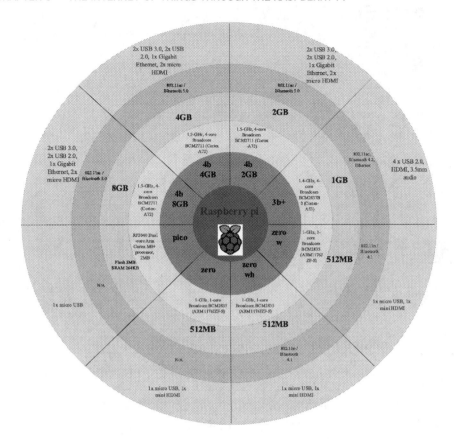

Figure 5-1. *Raspi-configurations and facilities in different versions*

An individual Raspberry Pi (RPi) can be combined to form a cluster, which divides the work and makes computing faster. This chapter focuses on creating basic cluster computing with RPis.

Cluster Computing with Raspberry Pi Zero W

Message Passing Interface (MPI)

A Message Passing Interface (MPI) [2] is a communication interface for parallel programming. It allows several machines connected by a network to run applications in parallel. Message passing applications often execute identical code on many processors, which then interact with one another through library calls that fall into a few broad categories.

- Calls for initiating, managing, and concluding communications

- Communication requests between two distinct operations (point-to-point)

- Communication requests among a group of procedures (collective)

- Methods for creating custom data types

In this chapter,

- A simple two-cluster Raspberry Pi W is created.

- MPI programming with Python is discussed.

- Simple MPI loads in two clusters are executed, and performance is monitored.

Networking with RPis for Simple MPI Scripts

Parallel computing [3] requires communication between cluster computers [4]. This can be achieved using either a wired or a wireless Ethernet. For cluster communications [5], the Raspberry Pi Zero W's wireless

LAN is utilized. Depending on the workload, a huge number of data may be transferred and engaged in a great deal of communication between the nodes; in this case, it may be preferable to utilize dedicated wired connections that offer substantially higher throughput. For instance, you can create wired connections between RPis using a Gigabit Ethernet switch. A suitable RPi should be converted on such occasions, such as the new 4B, which features a Gigabit Ethernet connection for wired communications. RPi communication was covered in the previous chapters.

This chapter uses a Dynamic Host Configuration Protocol (DHCP) configuration.

The SSH key generation is done through the following.

ssh-keygen -t rsa

The key sharing uses public keys through heterogeneous hosts.

ssh-copy-id <username@hostip>

The public keys from the host must be copied to all clients. The preceding command is run on each client to do this. Each client's IP address is given on the host computer, and each client's IP address is returned to the host.

MPI is installed by running the following scripts.

sudo apt install mpich python3-mpi4py

The following command tests the setup.

mpiexec -n 1 hostname

In the preceding command, the hostname is run on each node, and the result is returned. The ifconfig command finds the IP addresses for both RPis.

The following command needs to be run on both RPis to finish testing.

mpiexec -n 2 --host <IP1,IP2> hostname

Simple MPI Programming

This section presents a simple example of MPI programming, specifically, a simple Blink and Hello World program using MPI algorithms.

In C, MPI_Init and MPI_Finalize initialize and close interprocess communications, respectively. In between, the parallel algorithm jobs and the utilization of MPI constructs—such as size (the number of nodes in the cluster), rank (your position within the cluster, which might serve the ID), and node name—are performed.

The below code snippet showcase the simple MPI programming.

Listing 5-1. Simple MPI C Program

//C code

```
#include <mpi.h>
#include <stdio.h>

int main(int argc, char *argv[])
{
  int siz, r, length;
  char name[MPI_MAX_PROCESSOR_NAME];
#if defined(MPI_VERSION) && (MPI_VERSION>=2)
  int provided;
  MPI_Init_thread(&argc, &argv, MPI_THREAD_MULTIPLE, &
  provided);
#else
  MPI_Init(&argc, &argv);
#endif

  MPI_Comm_size(MPI_COMM_WORLD, &siz);
  MPI_Comm_rank(MPI_COMM_WORLD, &r);
  MPI_Get_processor_name(name, & length);
```

```
printf("Hello, World! I am process %d of %d on %s.\n", r,
siz, name);
MPI_Finalize();
return 0;
}
```

Code snippet showcassing MPI program.

Listing 5-2. Simple MPI Python Program

\\ Python Script
```
from mpi4py import MPI
import sys

siz = MPI.COMM_WORLD.Get_size()
r = MPI.COMM_WORLD.Get_rank()
name = MPI.Get_processor_name()

sys.stdout.write("IoT, I am process %d of %d on %s.\n"
%(r,siz,name))

$ mpiexec -n 2 --host 191.168.1.110,191.168.1.111 python3
mpiiot.py
IoT, I am process 0 of 2 on proto0.
IoT, I am process 1 of 2 on proto1.
```

Types of Communication in Cluster Computing

Every piece of communication has tags [6] that give the receiver a way to recognize the message so it can decide how to act. The two types of communication between clients are *blocking* and *non-blocking*. The differences depend on how you want them to work. Most of the time, blocking is the communication type used between systems in a cluster. These functions block the caller until the receiver doesn't send back the data that was sent in parallel. So, the sender program won't keep running while it waits for the results it needs to keep going.

Generic Python objects can talk to each other through the send(), recv(), and sendrecv() methods. On the other hand, methods like Send() and Recv() send and receive large data arrays, such as NumPy arrays. Some types of calculations may need to be done faster, which is achieved by making sure that the systems can talk to each other without waiting for a response. This means they can send and share data for calculation without waiting for a reply.

MPI also has functions that don't block this kind of communication. A call-reception function starts the action, and a control function lets you determine if such a request was completed. The functions for getting calls are lsend() and lrecv (). These functions give back a Request object, which is a unique way to identify the operation that was asked for. Once this operation has been sent, you can use control functions like Test(), Wait(), and Cancel() from the Request class to see how well it works.

Persistent Communication

Non-blocking communication requests are run repeatedly since they are in a loop. Using persistent communications can improve the code's performance in these situations. Send init() and Recvinit() are the functions of the mpi4py module that takes care of this job. They are part of the Comm class, and when they return a request object, they make a persistent request.

Broadcasting

In broadcasting, the master node communicates the data to all the other connected nodes. Figure 5-2 illustrates the same copy of the data communicated to all the nodes in the cluster.

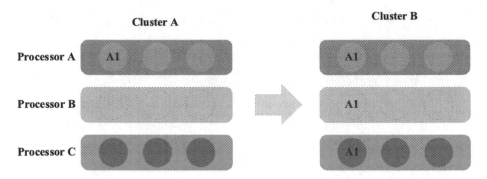

Figure 5-2. *Broadcasting data in the cluster*

Listing 5-3 is the code for broadcasting.

Listing 5-3. Broadcasting.py

```
from mpi4py import MPI

com = MPI.COMM_WORLD
r = comm.Get_rank()

if r == 0;
  info={'key1': [1, 2, 1+2j],
        'key2':('111','aaa')}
else:
  info = None
info = com.bcast(data, root=0)
print('from'+str(r))
print(info)
```

The code must be copied to all the cluster members in the network to broadcast the data.

Scattering

Scattering is a way for the master node to break up a data structure like a list and send each part to a different system in the cluster as a separate message. Figure 5-3 showcases the scattering of the data between the clusters.

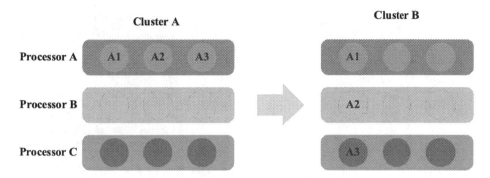

Figure 5-3. *Scattering data to clusters*

The code in Listing 5-4 must be copied to all the cluster members in the network.

Listing 5-4. Scatter.py

```
from mpi4py import MPI

com = MPI.COMM_WORLD
siz = comm.Get_size()
r = comm.Get_rank()

if r == 0;
  info = [(i+1)**2 for i in range(siz)]
else:
  info = None
info = com.scatter(info, root=0)
assert info == (r+1)**2
```

Gathering

Gathering is almost the polar opposite of scattering. In this instance, the master node is initialized and receives all data from the other cluster nodes. Figure 5-4 shows the gathering mechanism in clusters.

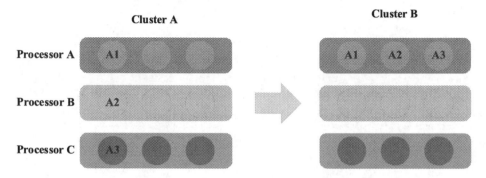

Figure 5-4. *The gathering concept in a cluster*

Listing 5-5 gathers all the cluster members.

Listing 5-5. Gather.py

```
from mpi4py import MPI

com = MPI.COMM_WORLD
siz = comm.Get_size()
r = comm.Get_rank()

info = (r+1)**2
info = com.gather(info, root=0)
if r == 0;
  for i in range(siz);
    assert info[i] == (i+1)**2
else:
  assert info is None
```

A Simple Web Service–Based Home Automation Using a Flask Server

Because it doesn't require any specific tools or libraries, Flask is referred to as a *micro framework* [7]. It does not have a database abstraction layer, form validation, and other components that third-party libraries commonly provide. However, Flask provides extensions that may extend application functionality as if it were built-in.

This chapter uses a Raspberry Pi as a local web server to operate three of its GPIOs programmed as output (working as actuators) and monitor two of its GPIOs written as input via a simple webpage (sensors).

Figure showcase the simple local network based GPIO activation and automation.

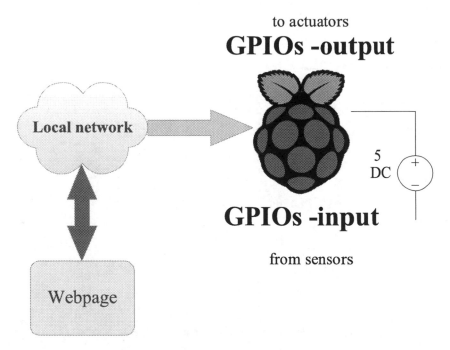

Figure 5-5. *Automation using a local network*

The following installs Flask.

```
apt-get install python3-flask
```

It creates a tree folder that includes the following.

```
/rpiWbserver
   /stat
   /templ
```

Run the Python script shown in Listing 5-6 to check the button press in the Flask web server.

Listing 5-6. Simple Flask Python Program

```python
import RPi.GPIO as GPIO
from flask import Flask, render_template
app = Flask(__name__)
GPIO.setmode(GPIO.BCM)
GPIO.setwarnings(False)
but = 20
but = GPIO.LOW
GPIO.setup(but, GPIO.IN)

@app.route("/")
def index():
    # Read Sensors Status
    but = GPIO.input(but)
    templateData = {
     'title' : 'GPIO status',
     'button'  : but,
     }
    return render_template('index.html', **templateData)
if __name__ == "__main__":
app.run(host='0.0.0.0', port=80, debug=True)
```

Listing 5-7. Simple Flask HTML Program

```
// Template code

<!DOCTYPE html>
<head>
<title>{{ title }}</title>
<link rel="stylesheet" href='../static/style.css'/>
</head>
<body>
    <h1>{{ title }}</h1>
<h2>Button pressed:  {{ button }}</h1>
</body>
</html>
```

Figure 5-6 shows the code's output.

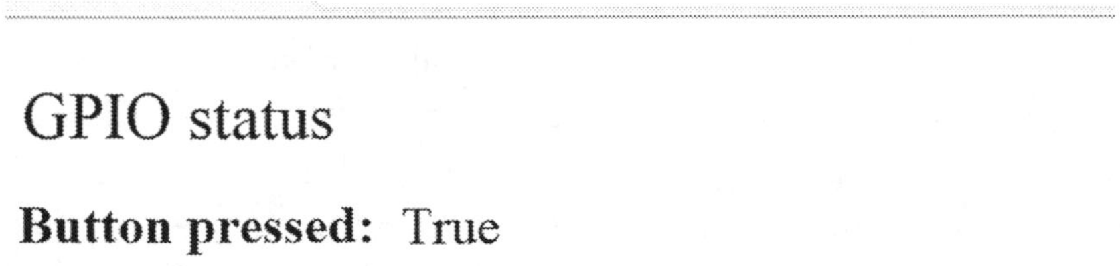

GPIO status

Button pressed: True

Figure 5-6. *Output in browser*

References

[1] G. R. Kanagachidambaresan, "Node-Red Programming and Page GUI Builder for Industry 4.0 Dashboard Design," *Role of Single Board Computers (SBCs) in Rapid IoT Prototyping*, Springer, 2021, pp. 121–140.

[2] Pavan Balaji, "Message Passing Interface," *Programming Models for Parallel Computing*, The MIT Press, 2015, pp.1–21.

[3] Rajkumar Buyya and Satish Narayana Srirama, "Wiley Series on Parallel and Distributed Computing," in *Fog and Edge Computing: Principles and Paradigms*, Wiley, 2019, pp. 1–4. doi: 10.1002/9781119525080.scard.

[4] D. Nageswari, R. Maheswar, and G. R. Kanagachidambaresan, "Performance analysis of cluster based homogeneous sensor network using energy efficient N-policy (EENP) model," *Cluster Computing,* vol. 22, pp. 12243–12250, 2019. https://doi.org/10.1007/s10586-017-1603-z.

[5] R. Maheswar et al., "CBPR: A Cluster-Based Backpressure Routing for the Internet of Things," *Wireless Personal Communications*, vol. 118, pp. 3167–3185, 2021. https://doi.org/10.1007/s11277-021-08173-0.

[6] D. V. Gadasin, A. V. Shvedov, and A. V. Koltsova, "Cluster Model for Edge Computing," 2020 International Conference on Engineering Management of Communication and Technology (EMCTECH), 2020, pp. 1–4. doi: 10.1109/EMCTECH49634.2020.9261538.

[7] A. S. Abhishek, M. Bhasker, and A. S. Ponraj, "IoT Based Control System for Home Automation," 2021 IEEE 2nd International Conference on Technology, Engineering, Management for Societal impact using Marketing, Entrepreneurship and Talent (TEMSMET), 2021, pp. 1–5. doi: 10.1109/TEMSMET53515.2021.9768686.

CHAPTER 6

Home Electrification and Node-RED

Node-RED [1] is a tool that uses flows and is written in Node.js. It takes up little memory and works on the Raspberry Pi, which makes it a great system for home automation projects [2]. Raspberry Pi comes with Node-RED installed, but you may need to upgrade it.

This chapter covers

- Monitoring home appliances through the IoT dashboard [3]

- Automating and operating home appliances through IoT devices [4]

The following command upgrades Node-RED.

```bash
bash <(curl -sL https://raw.githubusercontent.com/node-red/
linux-installers/master/deb/update-nodejs-and-nodered)
```

The execution of this command removes the older versions of Node-RED and Node.js. It updates to the latest Node-RED version and clears the npm cache. It can also set commands to work with other services.

Once Node-RED is installed, it can start from the command prompt. Figure 6-1 shows Node-RED starting in Raspberry Pi.

```
node-red start
```

© G. R. Kanagachidambaresan 2022
G. R. Kanagachidambaresan, *Internet of Things Using Single Board Computers*,
https://doi.org/10.1007/978-1-4842-8108-6_6

```
pi@raspberrypi:~ $ node-red-start

Start Node-RED

Once Node-RED has started, point a browser at http://192.168.1.226:1880
On Pi Node-RED works better with the Firefox or Chrome browser

Use    node-red-stop                        to stop Node-RED
Use    node-red-start                       to start Node-RED again
Use    node-red-log                         to view the recent log output
Use    sudo systemctl enable nodered.service  to autostart Node-RED at every boot
Use    sudo systemctl disable nodered.service to disable autostart on boot

To find more nodes and example flows - go to http://flows.nodered.org

Starting as a systemd service.
Started Node-RED graphical event wiring tool.
7 Jan 13:09:45 - [info]
Welcome to Node-RED
===================================================
7 Jan 13:09:45 - [info] Node-RED version: v1.2.7
7 Jan 13:09:45 - [info] Node.js  version: v10.23.1
7 Jan 13:09:45 - [info] Linux 5.4.51-v7+ arm LE
7 Jan 13:09:46 - [info] Loading palette nodes
7 Jan 13:09:48 - [info] Settings file  : /home/pi/.node-red/settings.js
7 Jan 13:09:48 - [info] Context store  : 'default' [module=memory]
7 Jan 13:09:48 - [info] User directory : /home/pi/.node-red
7 Jan 13:09:48 - [warn] Projects disabled : editorTheme.projects.enabled=false
7 Jan 13:09:48 - [info] Flows file     : /home/pi/.node-red/flows_raspberrypi.json
7 Jan 13:09:48 - [info] Creating new flow file
7 Jan 13:09:48 - [warn]
```

Figure 6-1. *Node-RED initialization in Raspberry Pi*

The Node-RED programming board and dashboard can be viewed within the local network. For example, if the Raspberry Pi IP is 192.169.0.101, the Node-RED programming dashboard can be viewed by entering 192.169.0.101:1880 in any computer browser connected to the local network. Figure 6-2 shows the programming dashboard.

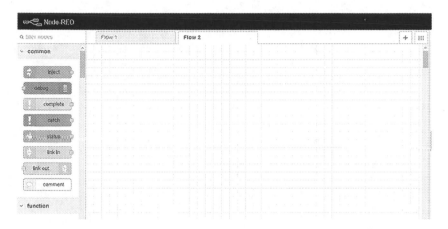

Figure 6-2. *Node-RED programming dashboard*

More palletes can be installed onto Node-RED from the "Manage-pallete" option on the right side of the programming pallete, as shown in Figure 6-3.

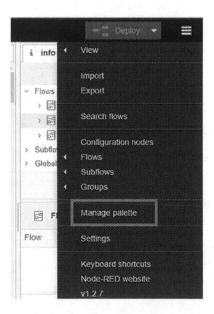

Figure 6-3. *Manage palette*

Figure 6-4 is a screenshot of the installation option in Node-RED.

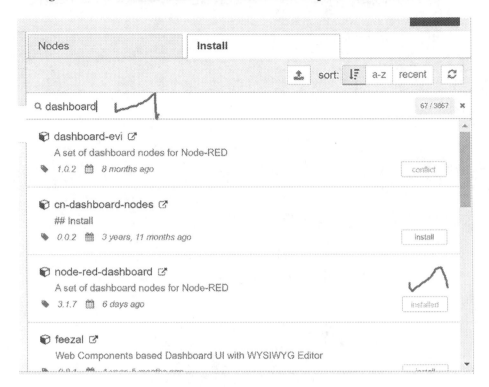

Figure 6-4.   *Dashboard pallete*

Once the Node-RED dashboard is installed, and the program is deployed, it can be viewed in the browser by typing 192.169.0.101:1880/ui. Figure 6-5 showcases the programming options in the browser.

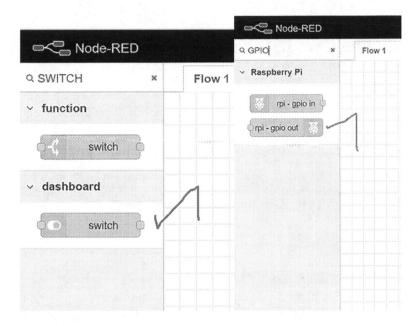

Figure 6-5. *Another dashboard screenshot*

The relays can be connected to Raspberry Pi with the proper power configurations. This chapter presents five applications controlled through the Node-RED platform. Figure 6-6 shows the drag-and-drop option for home automation. The circuit is configured to connect Raspberry Pi pins 36, 37, 38, and 40.

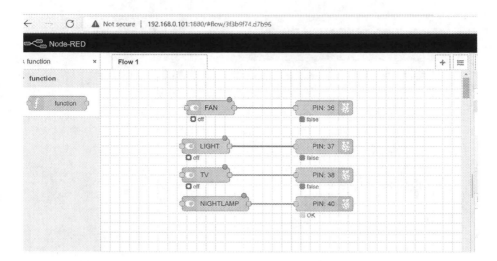

Figure 6-6. *Drag-and-drop program*

Figure 6-7 shows the home screen to control the relays connected via a local network. The same dashboard can be synchronized with Google Firebase or other cloud platforms to operate the device through the Internet.

Figure 6-7. *System browser dashboard view*

The user interface can also be viewed in a mobile browser connected to the same router, as shown in Figure 6-8.

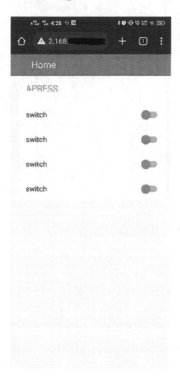

Figure 6-8. *Mobile browser screen*

Figure 6-9 shows relays connected to a Raspberry Pi Zero W.

Figure 6-9. *Real-time hardware connected to Raspberry Pi Zero W*

References

[1] A. Rajalakshmi and H. Shahnasser, "Internet of Things using Node-RED
and Alexa," in 2017 17th International Symposium on Communications
and Information Technologies (ISCIT), 2017, pp. 1–4. doi: 10.1109/
ISCIT.2017.8261194.

[2] M. Lekić and G. Gardašević, "IoT sensor integration to Node-RED
platform," in 2018 17th International Symposium INFOTEH-JAHORINA
(INFOTEH), 2018, pp. 1–5. doi: 10.1109/INFOTEH.2018.8345544.

[3] G. R. Kanagachidambaresan, "Node-Red Programming and Page
GUI Builder for Industry 4.0 Dashboard Design," in *Role of Single Board
Computers (SBCs) in Rapid IoT Prototyping*, Springer, 2021, pp. 121–140.

[4] R. K. Kodali and A. Anjum, "IoT-Based Home Automation Using Node-
RED," in 2018 Second International Conference on Green Computing
and Internet of Things (ICGCIoT), 2018, pp. 386–390. doi: 10.1109/
ICGCIoT.2018.8753085.

## CHAPTER 7

Supply Chain Management: Industry 4.0 and MQTT Applications

Introduction

Supply chain management [1] [2] and creating transparency between the shop floor workers and suppliers are achieved through Industry 4.0 standards. This chapter mainly deals with MQTT-based production system monitoring and software design with the help of single-board computers (SBCs) [3] [6]. An application is created in Python to send live information to the assembly unit from the Original Equipment Manufacturer (OEMs) [4] in a supply chain. A report must be generated at the end of the shift, and an automatic email must be sent to higher officials to maintain transparency throughout the supply chain and make production as economical and efficient as possible. Figure 7-1 illustrates the proposed model.

© G. R. Kanagachidambaresan 2022
G. R. Kanagachidambaresan, *Internet of Things Using Single Board Computers*,
https://doi.org/10.1007/978-1-4842-8108-6_7

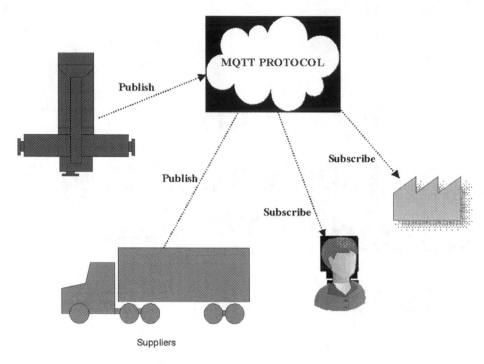

Figure 7-1. *MQTT-based supply chain data sharing*

The production line sensors are connected to the subscriber module and transmit data via the MQTT module. This chapter showcases a single MQTT-based publish-subscribe software that connects the OEMs in the supply chain [4].

Working Principle

The application's user interface is created with Python's Tkinter library. Individual modules are designed to complete certain tasks. The first is a timer module that counts down the time in decrements and alerts you when a shift is over, and an automatic email is sent to the appropriate authorities. The shift information is in an Excel file attached to the email. The smtplib and email packages in Python enable the automatic mail-send module.

A report can also be generated between shifts or before a shift ends. A Generate Report button activates the module. The pandas package saves the shift information in an Excel file named according to the date and time the report was prepared.

The numbers are published to an Internet MQTT server to acquire live updates of the good and bad counts from the manufacturing unit to the assembly unit. The HiveMQ MQTT server [5] is used in this situation. You can run functions and publish relevant values to the server using the paho-mqtt module in Python. Simultaneously, the assembly unit receives the values by subscribing to the topic in which they will be published. The assembly unit program, which uses Tkinter as its base UI, displays these values.

Publisher Source Code

```
1.   from tkinter import *
2.   from tkinter import ttk
3.   import tkinter as tk
4.   import time
5.   import random
6.   import pandas as pd
7.   import xlsxwriter
8.   from datetime import date, datetime
9.   from datetime import datetime
10.  import getpass
11.  import os
12.  import smtplib
13.  from email.message import EmailMessage
14.  import paho.mqtt.client as paho
15.  from paho import mqtt
16.
```

```
17.    qwe=[0,0,0,'0']
18.
19.    defon_connect(client, userdata, flags, rc,
       properties=None):
20.        print("Connection Success! Received with code
           %s."%rc)
21.
22.    # with this callback you can see if your publish was
       successful
23.    defon_publish(client, userdata, mid, properties=None):
24.        print("mid: "+str(mid))
25.
26.    # print which topic was subscribed to
27.    defon_subscribe(client, userdata, mid, granted_qos,
       properties=None):
28.        print("Subscribed: "+str(mid) +" "+str(granted_qos))
29.
30.    defon_message(client, userdata, msg):
31.        print(msg.topic+" "+str(msg.qos) +" "+str(msg.
           payload))
32.
33.    #Sends Automatic Mail once the Shift gets over
34.    defautomaticEmail():
35.        sender_email="mayoisnicee@gmail.com"
36.        sender_pass="Mayonnaise24"
37.        receiver_email="balakumarbk03@gmail.com"
38.
39.        msg=EmailMessage()
40.        msg['Subject'] ="REPORT"
41.        msg['From'] =sender_email
42.        msg['To'] =receiver_email
```

```
43.      msg.set_content('Shift Report Has Been Attached...')
         #to be filled
44.
45.
46.      #User Name
47.      user =getpass.getuser()
48.
49.      file_directory=["C:/Users/"+user +"/
         Documents/"+qwe[3] +  ".xlsx"]
50.
51.      forfileinfile_directory:
52.          with open(file, 'rb') as f:
53.              file_data=f.read()
54.              file_name=qwe[3]+'.xlsx'
55.              print("filename",file_name)
56.          msg.add_attachment(file_data,
             maintype='application',
57.          subtype='octet-stream', filename=file_name)
58.
59.
60.      with smtplib.SMTP_SSL("smtp.gmail.com", 465)
         as smtp:
61.          smtp.login(sender_email,sender_pass)
62.          smtp.send_message(msg)
63.      Label(root, text='Report Generated!', font ='arial
         15 bold').place(x=800, y=450)
64.      print("Mail Sent!")
65.
66.  defvals(count,good,bad):
67.      qwe[0] =count; qwe[1] =good; qwe[2] =bad
68.
```

```
69.    #Generates the current report when the Generate Report
       Button is clicked.
70.    defgenerateReport(): #(t,number,name,count,good,bad):
71.        #Date Time
72.        now =datetime.now()
73.        dt_string=now.strftime("%B %d %Y,%H-%M-%S")
74.        qwe[3] =dt_string
75.        #User Name
76.        user =getpass.getuser()
77.
78.        count_val,good_val,bad_val,shift_dt=[0],[0],[0],[0]
79.
80.        count_val[0] =qwe[0]
81.        good_val[0] =qwe[1]
82.        bad_val[0] =qwe[2]
83.        shift_dt[0] =dt_string
84.
85.        df=pd.DataFrame({'Shift Time':shift_dt[0],
86.                        'Shift Duration(secs)':t.get(),
87.                        'Shift Number':number.get(),
88.                        'Supervisor':name.get(),
89.                        'Production Count':count_val,
90.                        'Good Products':good_val,
91.                        'Defected Products':bad_val})
92.
93.        writer =pd.ExcelWriter(r"C:\Users\\"+ user +
           "\Documents\\" + dt_string +  ".xlsx")
94.
95.        # Convert the dataframe to an XlsxWriter
           Excel object.
```

```
96.      df.to_excel(writer, sheet_
         name='Sheet1',index =False)
97.      workbook  =writer.book
98.      worksheet =writer.sheets['Sheet1']
99.      worksheet.set_column('A:G',25)
100.     writer.save()
101.     print("Report Generated Successfully on "+dt_string)
102.
103.
104.
105.  #Shift Runtime
106.  defshiftRun():
107.      l =[]
108.      time_sec=int(t.get())
109.      count =0; good =0; bad =0
110.      whiletime_sec:
111.          mins, secs=divmod(time_sec, 60)
112.          timeformat='{:02d}:{:02d}'.format(mins, secs)
113.          #print(timeformat, end='\r')
114.          l.append(timeformat)
115.          #print(l[-1])
116.          count +=1
117.          ifrandom.randint(0,1):
118.              good +=1
119.          else:
120.              bad +=1
121.          Label(root, text=l[-1], font ='arial 15 bold').
              place(x=800, y=50)
122.          Label(root, text="Production Count:
              "+str(count), font ='arial 20 bold').
              place(x=20, y=360)
```

```
123.            Label(root, text="Good: "+str(good), font
                ='arial 20 bold').place(x=20, y=400)
124.            Label(root, text="Defects: "+str(bad), font
                ='arial 20 bold').place(x=20, y=440)
125.            client.publish("test/Bosch_
                Good",payload=str(good),qos=0)
126.            time.sleep(1)
127.            time_sec-=1
128.            root.update()
129.
130.            vals(count,good,bad)
131.        Label(root, text='Shift Ended!', font ='arial 15
            bold').place(x=800, y=80)
132.        generateReport()
133.        automaticEmail()
134.
135.    try:
136.        client =paho.Client(client_id="", userdata=None,
            protocol=paho.MQTTv5)
137.        client.on_connect=on_connect
138.
139.        # enable TLS
140.        client.tls_set(tls_version=mqtt.client.ssl.
            PROTOCOL_TLS)
141.
142.        client.username_pw_set("industry4.0", "Qwerty@123")
143.        client.connect("1d1587d792b6466fa8f2db432d9d3db2.
            s1.eu.hivemq.cloud", 8883)
144.
145.        client.on_message=on_message
146.        client.on_subscribe=on_subscribe
```

```
147.        client.on_publish=on_publish
148.
149.        root =Tk()
150.        root.geometry('1000x500')
151.        #production_name = input("Production Name(Eg: Bulb/
            Indicator/Housing/Electrical): ")
152.        Label(root, text ='Indicator Production', font
            ='arial 20 bold').pack()
153.
154.        #Starting Protocols
155.        Label(root, font ='arial 15 bold', text ='Set
            Time').place(x =20,y =50)
156.        t =Entry(root,width=15)
157.        t.place(x=180, y=55)
158.        Label(root, font ='arial 15 bold', text ='Shift
            Number').place(x =20,y =80)
159.        number =Entry(root,width=15)
160.        number.place(x=180, y=85)
161.        Label(root, font ='arial 15 bold', text
            ='Supervisor').place(x =20,y =110)
162.        name =Entry(root,width=15)
163.        name.place(x=180,y=115)
164.
165.        #Start Button
166.        Button(root, text='START', bd='5', command
            =shiftRun, font ='arial 10 bold').place(x=80, y=160)
167.
168.        #Generate Report Button
169.        Button(root, text='Generate Report', bd='5',
            command =generateReport, font ='arial 10 bold').
            place(x=800, y=400)
170.
```

```
171.

172.        #Quit Button
173.        ttk.Button(root, text="Quit", command=root.destroy).
           place(x=450,y=450)
174.        root.mainloop()
175.        print("Press 'Ctrl+C' to close the application.")
176.        client.loop_forever()

177.

178.

179.    exceptKeyboardInterrupt:
180.            print("Byeeee!!")
181.            pass
```

Subscriber Source Code

```
1.     importtime
2.     importpaho.mqtt.client as paho
3.     frompahoimportmqtt
4.     fromtkinterimport*
5.     fromtkinterimportttk
6.     importtkinter as tk

7.

8.

9.

10.    # setting callbacks for different events to see if it
       works, print the message etc.
11.    defon_connect(client, userdata, flags, rc,
       properties=None):
12.        print("Connection Success! Received with code %s."%rc)

13.
```

```
14.    # with this callback you can see if your publish was
       successful
15.    def on_publish(client, userdata, mid, properties=None):
16.        print("mid: "+str(mid))
17.
18.    # print which topic was subscribed to
19.    def on_subscribe(client, userdata, mid, granted_qos,
       properties=None):
20.        print("Subscribed: "+str(mid) +" "+str(granted_qos))
21.
22.    # print message, useful for checking if it was successful
23.    def on_message(client, userdata, msg):
24.        print(msg.topic+" "+str(msg.qos) +" "+str(msg.
           payload))
25.        topic =msg.topic
26.        payload =msg.payload
27.        if'Crompton_Good'in topic:
28.            #print("Update Crompton Label: ",payload)
29.            Label(root, text ='Crompton Production:
               '+str(payload) , font ='arial 20 bold').
               place(x=40,y=200)
30.
31.        elif'Bosch_Good'in topic:
32.            #print("Update Bosch Label: ",payload)
33.            Label(root, text ='Bosch Production:
               '+str(payload), font ='arial 20 bold').
               place(x=40,y=80)
34.        root.update()
35.
36.
37.    # using MQTT version 5 here, for 3.1.1: MQTTv311,
       3.1: MQTTv31
```

```
38.   # userdata is user defined data of any type, updated by
      user_data_set()
39.   # client_id is the given name of the client
40.   client =paho.Client(client_id="", userdata=None,
      protocol=paho.MQTTv5)
41.   client.on_connect=on_connect
42.
43.   # enable TLS for secure connection
44.   client.tls_set(tls_version=mqtt.client.ssl.PROTOCOL_TLS)
45.   # set username and password
46.   client.username_pw_set("industry4.0", "Qwerty@123")
47.   # connect to HiveMQ Cloud on port 8883 (default for MQTT)
48.   client.connect("1d1587d792b6466fa8f2db432d9d3db2.s1.eu.
      hivemq.cloud", 8883)
49.
50.   # setting callbacks, use separate functions like above
      for better visibility
51.   client.on_subscribe=on_subscribe
52.   client.on_message=on_message
53.   client.on_publish=on_publish
54.
55.   # subscribe to all topics of encyclopedia by using the
      wildcard "#"
56.   client.subscribe("sensor1/#", qos=0)
57.
58.   root =Tk()
59.   root.geometry('1000x500')
60.   #production_name = input("Production Name(Eg: Bulb/
      Indicator/Housing/Electrical): ")
61.   Label(root, text ='Assembly Unit', font ='arial 20
      bold').pack()
```

```
62.
63.    #ttk.Button(root, text="Quit", command=root.destroy).
       place(x=450,y=450)
64.    client.loop_forever()
```

A simple Python-based dashboard is created with Tkinter, and MQTT is created [7]. Figure 7-2 shows the publisher, providing the production value to the centralized dashboard through the MQTT approach. The data is shared through the IPv4 protocol via the HiveMQ MQTT server. The production data for every shift is mailed, and the same can be downloaded as a PDF through this Python application.

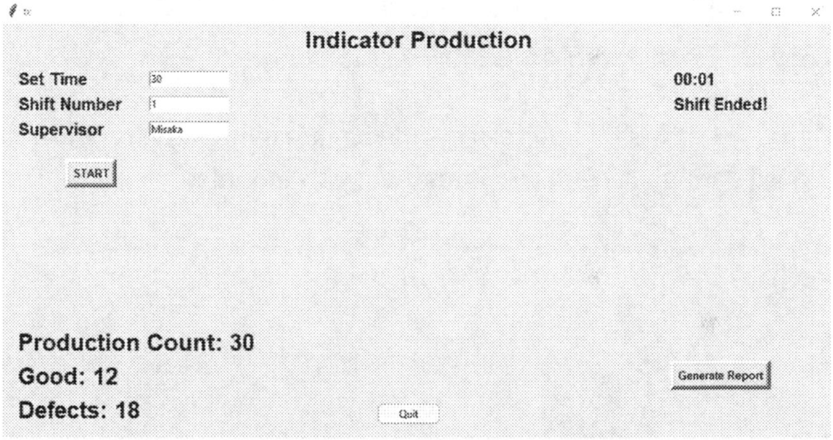

Figure 7-2. *Supplier dashboard showcasing production activity*

Figure 7-3 shows the full dashboard of the host industries. The production count, including both the good and the defective products, is tabulated to provide the shop floor output.

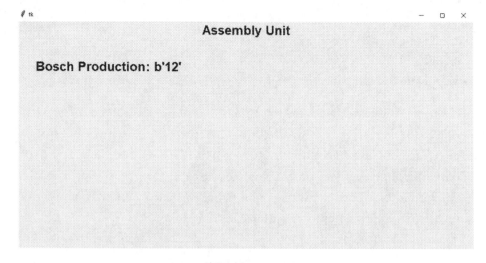

Figure 7-3. Production and consumer dashboard

Figure 7-4 shows the round-trip time it takes to update the consumer dashboard through 3G and 4G communication modules.

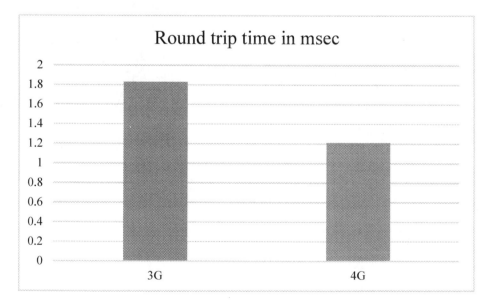

Figure 7-4. Round-trip time execution between 3G and 4G

Summary

This chapter discussed Python-based supply chain management through the MQTT protocol. The data is shared in 3G and 4G modules, and the response time is recorded for delay analysis. Image processing–based kit design for Industry 4.0 is discussed in the next chapter.

References

[1] Devendra A. Patil, "The Study of Industry 4.0 and Its Impact on Supply Chain Management," *International Research Journal of Engineering and Technology*, vol. 7, 2020.

[2] Abhijeet Ghadge, Merve Er Kara, Hamid Moradlou, and Mohit Goswami, "The impact of Industry 4.0 implementation on supply chains," *Journal of Manufacturing Technology Management*, March 2020.

[3] G. R. Kanagachidambaresan, *Role of Single Board Computers (SBCs) in Rapid IoT Prototyping*, Springer, 2021.

[4] Gourinath Banda, Chaitanya Krishna Bommakanti, and Harsh Mohan, "One IoT: an IoT protocol and framework for OEMs to make IoT-enabled devices forward compatible," *Journal of Reliable Intelligent Environments*, vol. 2, 2016, pp. 131–144.

[5] Biswajeeban Mishra and Attila Kertesz, "The Use of MQTT in M2M and IoT Systems: A Survey," *IEEE Access*, vol. 8, 2020.

[6] Jonathan Álvarez Ariza and Heyson Baez, "Understanding the role of single-board computers in engineering and computer science education: A systematic literature review," *Computer Applications in Engineering Education*, 2021.

[7] G. R. Kanagachidambaresan, "Node-Red Programming and Page GUI Builder for Industry 4.0 Dashboard Design," in *Role of Single Board Computers (SBCs) in Rapid IoT Prototyping*, Springer, 2021, pp. 121–140.

## CHAPTER 8

Raspberry Pi–Based Go/No-Go Kit Design Using the RPi Camera and Image Processing Algorithms

Introduction

Image-based recommendation systems [1] [2] are widely used in many industries to approve completed products and validate the products supplied by their suppliers. These consumer industries share specifications, and in many cases, they share the precise tool to operate and measure so that the quality of the product is high. High-quality products provide a high mean time to fail, often increasing customer and consumer trust. The devices and products in industries differ, and it is difficult to design an image processing–based recommendation system. With improvements in single-board computers and with the help of Python programs [3], it is easy to build a custom tool to monitor and validate production activities.

© G. R. Kanagachidambaresan 2022
G. R. Kanagachidambaresan, *Internet of Things Using Single Board Computers*,
https://doi.org/10.1007/978-1-4842-8108-6_8

Although a visual inspection with the naked eye is possible, it is often error-prone and costly: eyes tire, and working time is expensive. On the other hand, a mechanical test is often accompanied by complex calibration, which entails setting up and adjusting all software and hardware parameters to detect every error. Furthermore, changes to the product or materials necessitate recalibration. With the traditional rule-based approach, a programmer or an image processor must create custom rules for a system to explain how to detect errors. This is a difficult and often unsolvable Herculean task with a high variance of errors. All of this can take a significant amount of time and money. A quality inspection should be as efficient, simple, dependable, and cost-effective as possible.

In artificial vision [4], defect detection and classification are two subjects that must be approached as different challenges. Most digital image processing challenges come when researchers seek to imitate or replace human vision and decision-making techniques with artificial approaches. The overall purpose of replicating human vision is to detect and classify a subject; these two goals are interdependent. The two primary areas of artificial visual processing literature are visual processing algorithms, which are re-creations of human vision, and classifiers, which are redesigned human decision-making approaches. This book addresses both categories. But, instead of providing a comprehensive overview of all visual processing methods, the focus is on specific solutions that are closely related to visual processing methods, namely visual inspection techniques for metallic, ceramic, and textile surfaces in industrial applications.

In an industrial production line, quality monitoring is of the utmost importance [5]. Currently, numerous methods are utilized to evaluate the quality of a product or the outcome of a process. As depicted in Figure 8-1, quality control procedures can be classed as destructive or non-destructive, depending on the approach employed to discover a fault on a surface or volume. Non-destructive testing (NDT) observes a component

226

to find a problem without taking samples or harming it irreparably. The classifications of NDTs are a visual-based method, dye penetrant inspection, radiography, ultrasonic testing, eddy current technique, and thermography. They are predominantly employed in the realm of aviation.

Artificial intelligence, fuzzy math, expert systems, and fault tree analysis are classical fault detection methods derived from signal processing. The sensor embedded in the signal acquisition card limits the data quality for those approaches. In a real-world scenario, external elements such as heat, humidity, and electromagnetic radiation affect the sensor. As a result, sensor failure is one of the most common reasons for system failure in industrial robots [6].

In the automotive industry, industrial robots are used for welding, spraying, handling, and other applications. For each type of robot, manufacturers from Japan, Germany, the United States, and China provide a variety of models. Robot communication protocols are inherently complicated, and no single consistent standard exists.

Furthermore, because the interior environment's electromagnetic interference shielding is often disregarded, thermal radiation and other influences might cause erroneous measurements with the monitoring system embedded in the execution system. Other variables that contribute to robot failure, besides signal interference, include device aging, metal fatigue, and a lack of maintenance.

Industrial robots [7] [8] are a significant production tool for intelligent manufacturing and advanced industry. India is a significant manufacturing nation with many industrial robots in use. Unfortunately, industrial robots may mistakenly hurt surrounding workers while functioning at high intensity, high workload, and for lengthy periods of time, resulting in irreversible losses. The typical defect detection approach for robots mostly depends on the sensors, signal processing, and mathematical analysis.

The following are the disadvantages of such a system due to it being pricey and sensitive to sensor readings.

- The external environment can disrupt sensor data. Dust, water vapor, electromagnetic radiation, aging, and shell corrosion can cause sensor misinterpretation and failure.

- The communication protocols of various types of robots are complex and inconsistent. Industrial robots are available in a wide range of shapes, sizes, and brands. Because each manufacturer has designed its own communication protocol, it's impossible to design a general detection approach that applies to most types of industrial robots.

- Because the monitoring and execution systems are interconnected, the two systems regularly interact, resulting in oversizing, hybridity, and system interference.

- Industrial robot motors, arms, end effectors, and other locations have many sensors, resulting in expensive robot repair and maintenance costs.

Figure 8-1 illustrates an Industry 4.0–based specification validation system. The suppliers' products are moved in a conveyer mechanism and verified in a camera-based chamber. The camera chamber is connected to the Raspberry Pi and RPi camera to photograph the supplier's products. The products are photographed using the OpenCV-Python platform, and the specifications are validated with the standard image specifications. This chapter features car accessories milled and drilled by a supplier for further processing.

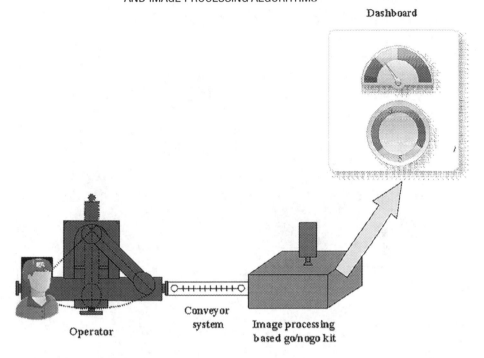

Figure 8-1. *Image processing–based go/no-go kit for Industry 4.0*

Figure 8-2 provides the GUI design and user interface to classify the drill hole with standard-size coins. The permissible amount of tolerance to accept the job piece is 0.9%. When the image-based classification identifies the amount of tolerance with a 96% confidence level, the output is communicated to the servo mechanism with GPIO pins to move the job piece further into the conveyer system for additional machining/assembly. The GUI is designed with the Tkinter package. Figure 8-2 shows the size of the hole measured by the classification model.

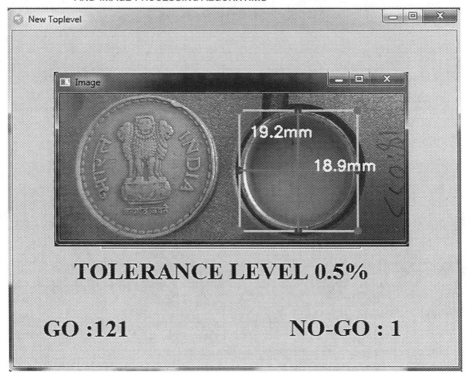

Figure 8-2. *GUI design using Python*

Below code illustrates the python code for dimension verification.

Listing 8-1. Support module 1

```
import sys

try:
    import Tkinter as tk
except ImportError:
    import tkinter as tk

try:
    import ttk
    py3 = False
```

```python
except ImportError:
    import tkinter.ttk as ttk
    py3 = True

import industry_support
def vp_start_gui():
    '''Starting point when module is the main routine.'''
    global val, w, root
    root = tk.Tk()
    top = Toplevel1 (root)
    industry_support.init(root, top)
    root.mainloop()

w = None
def create_Toplevel1(rt, *args, **kwargs):
    '''Starting point when module is imported by
    another module.
        Correct form of call: 'create_Toplevel1(root, *args,
        **kwargs)' .'''
    global w, w_win, root
    #rt = root
    root = rt
    w = tk.Toplevel (root)
    top = Toplevel1 (w)
    industry_support.init(w, top, *args, **kwargs)
    return (w, top)

def destroy_Toplevel1():
    global w
    w.destroy()
    w = None
```

```python
class Toplevel1:
    def __init__(self, top=None):
        '''This class configures and populates the
        toplevel window.
            top is the toplevel containing window.'''
        _bgcolor = '#d9d9d9'  # X11 color: 'gray85'
        _fgcolor = '#000000'  # X11 color: 'black'
        _compcolor = '#d9d9d9' # X11 color: 'gray85'
        _ana1color = '#d9d9d9' # X11 color: 'gray85'
        _ana2color = '#ececec' # Closest X11 color: 'gray92'
        top.geometry("600x450+342+122")
        top.minsize(116, 1)
        top.maxsize(1284, 782)
        top.resizable(1, 1)
        top.title("New Toplevel")
        top.configure(background="#d9d9d9")

        self.Canvas1 = tk.Canvas(top)
        self.Canvas1.place(relx=0.217, rely=0.067,
        relheight=0.518, relwidth=0.588)
        self.Canvas1.configure(background="#d9d9d9")
        self.Canvas1.configure(borderwidth="2")
        self.Canvas1.configure(insertbackground="black")
        self.Canvas1.configure(relief="ridge")
        self.Canvas1.configure(selectbackground="blue")
        self.Canvas1.configure(selectforeground="white")

        self.Label1 = tk.Label(top)
        self.Label1.place(relx=0.067, rely=0.778, height=21,
        width=100)
        self.Label1.configure(background="#d9d9d9")
```

```python
        self.Label1.configure(disabledforeground="#a3a3a3")
        self.Label1.configure(foreground="#000000")
        self.Label1.configure(text='''GO COUNT    20''')

        self.Label1_1 = tk.Label(top)
        self.Label1_1.place(relx=0.7, rely=0.778, height=21,
        width=100)
        self.Label1_1.configure(activebackground="#f9f9f9")
        self.Label1_1.configure(activeforeground="black")
        self.Label1_1.configure(background="#d9d9d9")
        self.Label1_1.configure(disabledforeground="#a3a3a3")
        self.Label1_1.configure(foreground="#000000")
        self.Label1_1.configure(highlightbackground="#d9d9d9")
        self.Label1_1.configure(highlightcolor="black")
        self.Label1_1.configure(text='''NO- GO COUNT    1''')
if __name__ == '__main__':
    vp_start_gui()
```

Below code shows the python code support module for size verification.

Listing 8-2. Supporting module 2

```python
#! /usr/bin/env python
#  -*- coding: utf-8 -*-
#
# Support module generated by PAGE version 5.4
#  in conjunction with Tcl version 8.6
#    Dec 16, 2021 10:34:30 PM +0530  platform: Windows NT

import sys

try:
    import Tkinter as tk
except ImportError:
    import tkinter as tk
```

```
try:
    import ttk
    py3 = False
except ImportError:
    import tkinter.ttk as ttk
    py3 = True

def init(top, gui, *args, **kwargs):
    global w, top_level, root
    w = gui
    top_level = top
    root = top

def destroy_window():
    # Function which closes the window.
    global top_level
    top_level.destroy()
    top_level = None

if __name__ == '__main__':
    import APRESS9
    industry.vp_start_gui()
```

Listing 8-3. Dimension Verification Module

```
# import the necessary packages
from scipy.spatial import distance as dist
from imutils import perspective
from imutils import contours
import numpy as np
import argparse
import imutils
import cv2
def midpoint(ptA, ptB):
```

```python
    return ((ptA[0] + ptB[0]) * 0.5, (ptA[1] + ptB[1]) * 0.5)
# construct the argument parse and parse the arguments
ap = argparse.ArgumentParser()
ap.add_argument("-i", "--image", required=True,
    help="path to the input image")
ap.add_argument("-w", "--width", type=float, required=True,
    help="width of the left-most object in the image (in
    inches)")
args = vars(ap.parse_args())

# load the image, convert it to grayscale, and blur it slightly
image = cv2.imread(args["image"])
scale_percent = 60 # percent of original size
width = int(image.shape[1] * scale_percent / 100)
height = int(image.shape[0] * scale_percent / 100)
dim = (width, height)

# resize image
image = cv2.resize(image, dim, interpolation = cv2.INTER_AREA)

gray = cv2.cvtColor(image, cv2.COLOR_BGR2GRAY)
gray = cv2.GaussianBlur(gray, (7, 7), 0)
# perform edge detection, then perform a dilation + erosion to
# close gaps in between object edges
edged = cv2.Canny(gray, 50, 100)
edged = cv2.dilate(edged, None, iterations=1)
edged = cv2.erode(edged, None, iterations=1)
# find contours in the edge map
cnts = cv2.findContours(edged.copy(), cv2.RETR_EXTERNAL,
    cv2.CHAIN_APPROX_SIMPLE)
cnts = imutils.grab_contours(cnts)
# sort the contours from left-to-right and initialize the
```

```python
# 'pixels per metric' calibration variable
(cnts, _) = contours.sort_contours(cnts)
pixelsPerMetric = None

# loop over the contours individually
for c in cnts:
    # if the contour is not sufficiently large, ignore it
    if cv2.contourArea(c) < 100:
        continue
    # compute the rotated bounding box of the contour
    orig = image.copy()
    box = cv2.minAreaRect(c)
    box = cv2.cv.BoxPoints(box) if imutils.is_cv2() else cv2.
    boxPoints(box)
    box = np.array(box, dtype="int")
    # order the points in the contour such that they appear
    # in top-left, top-right, bottom-right, and bottom-left
    # order, then draw the outline of the rotated bounding
    # box
    box = perspective.order_points(box)
    cv2.drawContours(orig, [box.astype("int")], -1, (0,
    255, 0), 2)
    # loop over the original points and draw them
    for (x, y) in box:
        cv2.circle(orig, (int(x), int(y)), 5, (0, 0, 255), -1)
        # unpack the ordered bounding box, then compute the
        midpoint
    # between the top-left and top-right coordinates,
    followed by
    # the midpoint between bottom-left and bottom-right
    coordinates
    (tl, tr, br, bl) = box
```

```python
(tltrX, tltrY) = midpoint(tl, tr)
(blbrX, blbrY) = midpoint(bl, br)
# compute the midpoint between the top-left and top-
right points,
# followed by the midpoint between the top-righ and
bottom-right
(tlblX, tlblY) = midpoint(tl, bl)
(trbrX, trbrY) = midpoint(tr, br)
# draw the midpoints on the image
cv2.circle(orig, (int(tltrX), int(tltrY)), 5, (255,
0, 0), -1)
cv2.circle(orig, (int(blbrX), int(blbrY)), 5, (255,
0, 0), -1)
cv2.circle(orig, (int(tlblX), int(tlblY)), 5, (255,
0, 0), -1)
cv2.circle(orig, (int(trbrX), int(trbrY)), 5, (255,
0, 0), -1)
# draw lines between the midpoints
cv2.line(orig, (int(tltrX), int(tltrY)), (int(blbrX),
int(blbrY)), (255, 0, 255), 2)
cv2.line(orig, (int(tlblX), int(tlblY)), (int(trbrX),
int(trbrY)), (255, 0, 255), 2)

# compute the Euclidean distance between the midpoints
dA = dist.euclidean((tltrX, tltrY), (blbrX, blbrY))
dB = dist.euclidean((tlblX, tlblY), (trbrX, trbrY))
# if the pixels per metric has not been initialized, then
# compute it as the ratio of pixels to supplied metric
# (in this case, inches)
```

```
    if pixelsPerMetric is None:
        pixelsPerMetric = dB / args["width"]

    # compute the size of the object
    dimA = dA / pixelsPerMetric
    dimB = dB / pixelsPerMetric
    # draw the object sizes on the image
    cv2.putText(orig, "{:.1f}mm".format(dimA),
        (int(tltrX - 65), int(tltrY + 35)), cv2.FONT_HERSHEY_
        SIMPLEX, 0.65, (255, 255, 255), 2)
    cv2.putText(orig, "{:.1f}mm".format(dimB),
        (int(trbrX - 60), int(trbrY)), cv2.FONT_HERSHEY_
        SIMPLEX, 0.65, (255, 255, 255), 2)
    # show the output image
    cv2.imshow("Image", orig)
    cv2.waitKey(0)
```

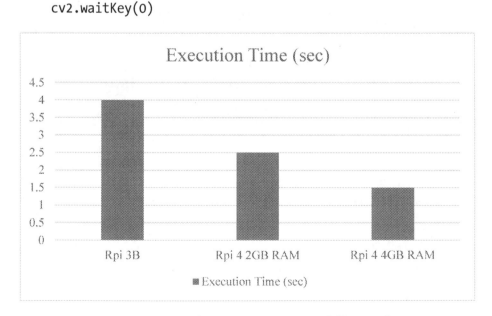

Figure 8-3. *Comparison of execution time in different devices*

Figure 8-3 compares the execution time of the code in different Raspberry Pi models. The Raspberry Pi 4 with 4 GB RAM executes fastest, and the Raspberry Pi 3 executes slower than the other models.

A smart farming–based project with single-board computers is discussed in the next chapter. Different water quality sensors and interfacing with the single-board computers and calibrations are also discussed.

References

[1] P. Yin and L. Zhang, "Image Recommendation Algorithm Based on Deep Learning," *IEEE Access*, vol. 8, 2020, pp. 132799–132807. doi: 10.1109/ ACCESS.2020.3007353.

[2] F. Ullah, B. Zhang, and R. U. Khan, "Image-Based Service Recommendation System: A JPEG-Coefficient RFs Approach," *IEEE Access*, vol. 8, 2020, pp. 3308–3318. doi: 10.1109/ACCESS.2019.2962315.

[3] A. Saxena, M. Tyagi, and P. Singh, "Digital Outing System Using RFID And Raspberry Pi with MQTT Protocol," 2018 3rd International Conference on Internet of Things: Smart Innovation and Usages (IoT-SIU), 2018, pp. 1–4. doi: 10.1109/IoT-SIU.2018.8519923.

[4] Y. Li and Y. Zhang, "Application Research of Computer Vision Technology in Automation," 2020 International Conference on Computer Information and Big Data Applications (CIBDA), 2020, pp. 374–377. doi: 10.1109/CIBDA50819.2020.00090.

[5] A. Kazemian, X. Yuan, O. Davtalab, and B. Khoshnevis, "Computer vision for real-time extrusion quality monitoring and control in robotic construction," *Automation in Construction*, vol. 101, May 2019, pp. 92–98.

[6] Karthick Thiyagarajan, Sarath Kodagoda, Linh Van Nguyen, and Ravindra Ranasinghe, "Sensor Failure Detection and Faulty Data Accommodation Approach for Instrumented Wastewater Infrastructures," *IEEE Access*, vol. 6.

[7] Tadeusz Mikolajczyk, "Manufacturing Using Robot," *Advanced Materials Research*, March 2012. doi: 10.4028/www.scientific.net/AMR.463-464.1643.

[8] Wanek Golnazarian and Ernest Hall, "Intelligent Industrial Robots," IMTS 2002 Manufacturing Conference, Sept. 2002. doi: 10.1201/9780203908587.ch6.5.

## CHAPTER 9

Programming Water-Quality Sensors

Introduction

Water quality [1] is mainly determined by various water quality parameters, such as the following.

- pH
- DO
- Turbidity
- Salinity
- TDS
- Water Temperature

Figure 9-1 showcases a pH sensor.

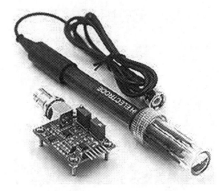

Figure 9-1. *Single board computer adaptable pH sensor*

Table 9-1 provides the specifications of a pH sensor.

The optimum levels in the parameters [2] listed in Table 9-1 make water more suitable for drinking and other purposes.

Table 9-1. *pH sensor specifications*

Measuring Range: 0 to 14.00 pH

Sensitivity: 0.002 pH

Stability: 0.02 pH per 24 hours, non-cumulative

Wetted Materials: PEEK, ceramic, titanium, glass, Viton, EDPM

 (optional: 316 stainless steel with 316SS body)

Temperature Compensation: Pt1000 RTD

Sensor Cable: 6 conductors (5 are used) plus 2 shields, 15 ft (4.6 m) length standard

Temperature Range: −5°C to +95°C (23°F to 203°F)

Pressure Range: 0 to 100 psig

Maximum Flow Rate: 10 ft (3 m) per second

Distance: 3,000 ft (914 m)

Sensor Body Options: 1″ NPT convertible, 1¼″ insertion, 1½″ or 2″ sanitary-style

Weight: 1 lb (0.45 kg)

Ideal drinking water conditions are listed in Table 9-2.

Table 9-2. *Water Quality Parameters for Drinking Water*

S.No.	Parameters	Drinking water IS 10500 : 2012	
		Permissible Limit	Maximum Limit
1	Odor	Agreeable	Agreeable
2	Taste	Agreeable	Agreeable
3	pH	6.5 to 8.5	No relaxation
4	TDS (mg/l)	500	2000
5	Hardness (as CaCO3) (mg/l)	200	600
6	Alkalinity (as CaCO3) (mg/l)	200	600
7	Nitrate (mg/l)	45	No relaxation
8	Sulfate (mg/l)	200	400
9	Fluoride (mg/l)	1	1.5
10	Chloride (mg/l)	250	1000
11	Turbidity (NTU)	5	10
12	Arsenic (mg/l)	0.01	0.05
13	Copper (mg/l)	0.05	1.5
14	Cadmium (mg/l)	0.003	No relaxation
15	Chromium (mg/l)	0.05	No relaxation
16	Lead (mg/l)	0.01	No relaxation
17	Iron (mg/l)	0.3	No relaxation
18	Zinc (mg/l)	5	15
19	Fecal Coliform (cfu)	0	0
20	E. Coli (cfu)	0	0

(*Source:* http://iitk.ac.in/iwd/wq/drinkingwater.htm)

The water quality parameters suitable for irrigation purposes are listed in Table 9-3.

Table 9-3. *Irrigation Water Quality Parameters*

Parameters	Unit Measure	Adequate for Irrigation	Warning	Extreme Restrictions
pH		$6.00 \div 8.00$	5.00–5.99 8.01–9.00	<5.00 >9.00
EC	$dS\,m^{-1}$	<0.70	0.70–6.50	>6.50
SAR		<3.00	3.00–9.00	>9.00
E. coli	mean number per 100 mL	<1000		>1000
Intestinal nematodes	arithmetic mean n. of eggs per litre	<1		>1
TSS	$mg\,L^{-1}$	<200	200–400	>400
HCO_3	$mg\,L^{-1}$	<150	150–300	>300
Fe	$mg\,L^{-1}$	<0.50	0.50–1.50	>1.50
Mn	$mg\,L^{-1}$	<0.10	0.10–1.50	>1.50
H_2S	$mg\,L^{-1}$	<0.50	0.50–2.00	>2.00

Figure 9-2 showcases a DO sensor which can be read through arduino and other single board computers.

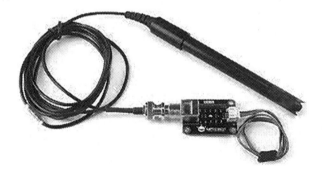

Figure 9-2. *DO sensor for single board computers*

Figure 9-3. *Temperature sensor*

244

Figure 9-4. *Turbidity sensor*

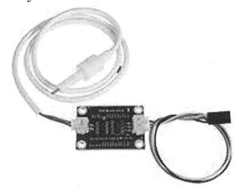

Figure 9-5. *TDS sensor*

Monitoring the important parameters of the water with sensor through arduino is discussed in Table 9-4.

Table 9-5 shows the water quality sensor interfacing with the Raspberry Pi and other python based single board computers.

Table 9-4. *Programming water quality sensors with arduino*

Sensors	Sensor Image	Voltage Range	Connectivity	Detection Range	Pin Configuration	Arduino Code
pH		+5V	Analog	0.0-14.0 pH	VCC-VCC GND-GND A0-A0	```int pH_Value;
float Voltage;

void setup()
{
  Serial.begin(9600);
  pinMode(pH_Value, INPUT);
}

void loop()
{
  pH_Value = analogRead(A0);
  Voltage = pH_Value * (5.0 / 1023.0);
  Serial.println(Voltage);
  delay(500);
}``` |

| DO | | +3.3V- +5.5V | Analog | 0-20mg/L | VCC-3.3V GND-GND Analog output-A1 | |

```
#include <Arduino.h>
#define VREF
5000//VREF(mv)
#define ADC_RES
1024//ADC Resolution

uint32_t raw;

void setup()
{
    Serial.
    begin(115200);
}

void loop()
{
    raw=analogRead(A1);
    Serial.
    println("raw:
\t"+String(raw)+"\
tVoltage(mv)"+String
(raw*VREF/ADC_RES));
    delay(1000);
}
```

(continued)

247

Table 9-4. (*continued*)

Sensors	Sensor Image	Voltage Range	Connectivity	Detection Range	Pin Configuration	Arduino Code
Turbidity		+5V	Analog	0% - 3.5%(0 -4550NTU)	VCC-5V GND-GND Analog output-A0	```void setup() {
Serial.begin(9600);
}
void loop() {
int sensorValue =
analogRead(A0);
float voltage =
sensorValue * (5.0 /
1024.0);
Serial.println
("Sensor Output
(V):");
Serial.println
(voltage);
Serial.println();
delay(1000);
}```

| Salinity | 5V | Analog | 0-50ppt (0-50,000ppm) | VCC-5V GND-GND A0-A0 | ```int potPin = 0;
float refvoltage = 5.0;
voidsetup()
{
Serial.begin(9600);
Serial.println("Sal
sensor ");
}
voidloop()
{
int samples = 20;
int aRead = 0;
for (int i = 0; i <
samples ; i++)
{
aRead +=
analogRead(potPin);
}
float voltage =
refvoltage * aRead/
(1023 * samples);``` |
| --- | --- | --- | --- | --- | --- |

(continued)

Table 9-4. (*continued*)

Sensors	Sensor Image	Voltage Range	Connectivity	Detection Range	Pin Configuration	Arduino Code
| | | | | | | ```
float ppt = 16.3 *
voltage;

Serial.print("Analog
in reading: ");
Serial.print(aRead);

Serial.print(" -
voltage: ");
Serial.
println(voltage , 3);

Serial.print(" -
Calculated ppt: ");
Serial.println(ppt,
2);
delay(500);
}
``` |
```

| TDS |  | 3.3V-5.5V | Analog | 0-1000ppm | VCC-5V
GND-GND
Analog output-any analog output | |

```
#include <EEPROM.h>
#include "GravityTDS.h"
#define TdsSensorPin A1
GravityTDS gravityTds;

float temperature =
25,tdsValue = 0;

void setup()
{
    Serial.begin(115200);
    gravityTds.
setPin(TdsSensorPin);
    gravityTds.
setAref(5.0);
    //reference voltage
on ADC, default 5.0V
on Arduino UNO
    gravityTds.
setAdcRange(1024);
    //1024 for 10bit ADC;
4096 for 12bit ADC
```

(continued)

Table 9-4. (*continued*)

Sensors	Sensor Image	Voltage Range	Connectivity	Detection Range	Pin Configuration	Arduino Code

						`gravityTds.begin();`
						`//initialization`
						`}`
						
						`void loop()`
						`{`
						`//temperature =`
						`readTemperature();`
						`//add your temperature`
						`sensor and read it`
						`gravityTds.set`
						`Temperature`
						`(temperature);`
						`// set the temperature`
						`and execute temperature`
						`compensation`
						`gravityTds.update();`
						`//sample and calculate`

```
tdsValue = gravityTds.
getTdsValue();
// then get the value
Serial.
print(tdsValue,0);
Serial.
println("ppm");
delay(1000);
}

#include <DHT.h>

//Constants
#define DHTPIN 2
// what pin we're
connected to
#define DHTTYPE DHT11
// DHT 11 (AM2302)
// Initialize DHT
sensor for normal
16mhz Arduino
DHT dht(DHTPIN,
DHTTYPE);
```

| Temperature | | 3V – 5V | Digital | 0 -50°C | VCC- 5V GND-GND Data-D2 |

(continued)

253

Table 9-4. (*continued*)

Sensors	Sensor Image	Voltage Range	Connectivity	Detection Range	Pin Configuration	Arduino Code
						```//Variables int chk; float hum; //Stores humidity value float temp; //Stores temperature value void setup() { Serial.begin(9600); dht.begin(); } void loop() { //Read data and store it to variables hum and temp hum = dht. readHumidity();```

```
temp= dht.
readTemperature();
  //Print temp and
humidity values to
serial monitor
  Serial.
print("Humidity: ");
  Serial.print(hum);
  Serial.print(" %,
Temp: ");
  Serial.print(temp);
  Serial.println("
Celsius");
  delay(2000);
  //Delay 2 sec.
  }
```

Table 9-5. Python based interface for water quality sensors

Sensors	Python Code
| pH | ```
import json, time, conf
from boltiot import Bolt, Sms #Import Sms and Bolt class from boltiot library

value1 = 0
value2 = 6.5
value3 = 7.5
value4 = 14

mybolt = Bolt(conf.API_KEY, conf.DEVICE_ID) #Create object to fetch data
sms = Sms(conf.SID, conf.AUTH_TOKEN, conf.TO_NUMBER, conf.FROM_NUMBER)
#Create object to send SMS
response = mybolt.serialRead('10')
print response

while True:
    print("Reading Sensor Value")
    response = mybolt.serialRead('10')   #Fetching the value from Arduino
    data = json.loads(response)
    ph_value = data['value'].rstrip()
    print("pH Valueis:"+str(data['value']))
``` |
```

```
try:
    if ph_value > value1 and ph_value < value2:
        print("Making request to send SMS")
        response = sms.send_sms("The liquid is ACIDIC. pH value of the liquid
        is:"+str(ph_value))
        print("Response recieved:"+ste(response.status))
    elif ph_value > value2 and ph_value < value3:
        print("Making request to send SMS")
        response = sms.send_sms("The liquid is NEUTRAL. pH value of the
        liquid is:"+str(ph_value))
        print("Response recieved:"+ste(response.status))
    elif ph_value > value3 and ph_value < value4:
        print("Making request to send SMS")
        response = sms.send_sms("The liquid is ALKALINE. pH value of the
        liquid is:"+str(ph_value))
        print("Response recieved:"+ste(response.status))
except Exception as e:
    print("Error occured: Below are the details")
    print(e)
time.sleep(100) #reads sensor value for every 100 seconds
```

(continued)

257

Table 9-5. (*continued*)

Sensors	Python Code
DO	
| turbidity | ```
Importtime
importboard
importbusio
importadafruit_ads1x15.ads1015asADS
fromadafruit_ads1x15.analog_inimportAnalogIn

# Create the I2C bus
i2c=busio.I2C(board.SCL,board.SDA)

# Create the ADC object using the I2C bus
ads=ADS.ADS1015(i2c)

# Create single-ended input on channel 0
chan=AnalogIn(ads,ADS.P0)

# Create differential input between channel 0 and 1
# chan = AnalogIn(ads, ADS.P0, ADS.P1)

print("{:>5}\t{:>5}".format("raw","v"))

whileTrue:
    print("{:>5}\t{:>5.3f}".format(chan.value,chan.voltage))
    time.sleep(0.5)
``` |
```

Salinity

TDS

```
import math
import sys
import time
from grove.adc import ADC

class GroveTDS:

    def __init__(self, channel):
        self.channel = channel
        self.adc = ADC()

    @property
    def TDS(self):
        value = self.adc.read(self.channel)
        if value != 0:
            voltage = value*5/1024.0
            tdsValue = (133.42/voltage*voltage*voltage-255.86*voltage*voltage+857
            .39*voltage)*0.5
            return tdsValue
        else:
            return 0
```

(continued)

259

Table 9-5. (*continued*)

Sensors	Python Code

```python
Grove = GroveTDS

def main():
    if len(sys.argv) < 2:
        print('Usage: {} adc_channel'.format(sys.argv[0]))
        sys.exit(1)

    sensor = GroveTDS(int(sys.argv[1]))
    print('Detecting TDS...')

    while True:
        print('TDS Value: {0}'.format(sensor.TDS))
        time.sleep(1)

if __name__ == '__main__':
    main()
```

(continued)

Temperature

```
import serial
import re
import csv
import numpy as np
import matplotlib.pyplot as plt
from drawnow import *

# Set path to my Arduino device
portPath = "/dev/tty.usbmodemfa411"
baud = 9600
sample_time = 0.1
sim_time = 10

# Initializing Lists
# Data Collection
data_log = []
line_data = []
```

Table 9-5. *(continued)*

Sensors   **Python Code**

```
# Establishing Serial Connection
connection = serial.Serial(portPath,baud)

# Calculating the length of data to collect based on the
# sample time and simulation time (set by user)
max_length = sim_time/sample_time

plt.ion() #Tell matplotlib you want interactive mode to plot live data

# Create a function that makes our desired plot
def makeFig():
    plt.ylim(15,35)
    plt.title('Temperatur Sensor Data')
    plt.grid(True)
    plt.ylabel('Temperatur C')
    plt.plot(data_log, 'ro-', label='Degrees C')

# Collecting the data from the serial port
while True:
    line = connection.readline()
    line_data = re.findall('\d*\.\d*',str(line))
```

```python
    line_data = filter(None,line_data)
    line_data = [float(x) for x in line_data]
    if len(line_data) > 0:
        print(line_data[0])
        if float(line_data[0]) > 0.0:
            drawnow(makeFig)
            plt.pause(.000001)
            data_log.append(line_data)
    if len(data_log) > max_length - 1:
        break

# Storing data_log in data.csv
with open('data.csv', 'w', newline='') as csvfile:
    for line in data_log:
        csvwrite = csv.writer(csvfile)
        csvwrite.writerow(line)
```

Creating water quality–based aquaculture is discussed in the next chapter. Water quality–based farming improves the feed conversion ratio and farmers' productivity, allowing lower risk/higher profits for farmers.

References

[1] A. N. Prasad, K. Mamun, F. Islam, and H. Haqva, "Smart Water Quality Monitoring System," IEEE, 2015. doi: 10.1109/APWCCSE.2015.7476234.

[2] Nayla Omer, "Water Quality Parameters," in *Water Quality: Science, Assessments and Policy*, IntechOpen, 2020. doi:10.5772/intechopen.89657.

CHAPTER 10

IoT-Based Shrimp Farming

Shrimp farming is an aquaculture business [1] that can occur in saltwater or freshwater [2]. Ocean shrimp farming is a very old industry popular in many Asian countries. Prior to ten years ago, shrimp were usually considered a second crop in traditional fish farming systems. The shrimp caught in salt beds, coastal paddy fields, or brackish water fishponds are left to grow until they are big enough to sell, and then they are harvested as a secondary crop. But in recent years, farmers have started growing shrimp as their main crop. Many farmers have made shrimp farms in their rice fields, fish ponds, and salt beds. Nowadays, most shrimp farmers [3] use modern methods to raise shrimp. A small piece of land can be used to make a lot of food.

Shrimp farming [4] in freshwater is also growing in popularity. In 2010, about 670,000 tons of freshwater prawns were raised around the world, the majority in China.

The influencing factors of shrimp farming are shown in Figure 10-1.

© G. R. Kanagachidambaresan 2022
G. R. Kanagachidambaresan, *Internet of Things Using Single Board Computers*,
https://doi.org/10.1007/978-1-4842-8108-6_10

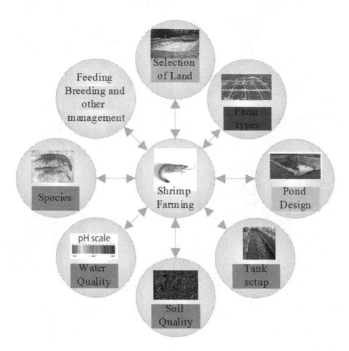

Figure 10-1. *Shrimp farming factors and parameters*

The key points of land selection include avoiding residential areas and accessibility to good electricity, water, and transportation. There are many ways to raise shrimp: in ponds made of soil, concrete tanks, plastic tanks, or any other type of water reservoir.

Organizations like the Central Institute of Brackishwater Aquaculture (CIBA) provide guidelines for shrimp pond setup [1]. Shrimp farming works best in a simple pond with enough water depth. Before preparing land for shrimp production, the types and texture of the soil in the chosen region must be studied. Soil samples from arbitrary locations (preferably up to a depth of 0.5 meters) are collected. Physical and chemical tests are conducted to evaluate the soil's acidity, organic load, fertility level, and physical makeup.

The presence of sufficient clay in the soil is essential for shrimp production. Sandy clay or sandy loam soil is regarded as suitable for agricultural development.

It's also important for a shrimp farming business [5] to keep the water clean. The physical, chemical, and biological properties of water are all part of its quality. The right pH level is a very important for a business that grows shrimp. The water should have a pH between 7.5 and 8.5. The dissolved oxygen level should not fall below 4 ppm. Shrimp feeding, breeding, and other management can be monitored through expertise and an automation process via IoT. This chapter focuses on the continuous monitoring of water-quality parameters [6].

A NodeMCU-based continuously monitoring [7] data buoy is constructed in this chapter. The device's architecture is illustrated in Figure 10-2.

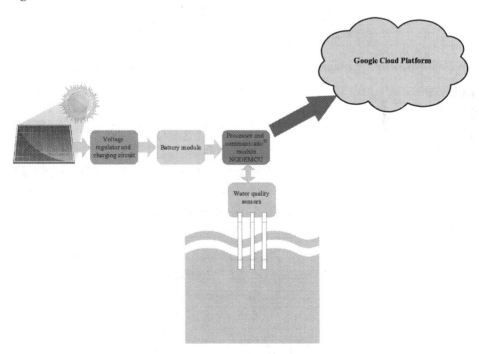

Figure 10-2. *The architecture of the design*

Figure 10-2 shows the data buoy constructed for continuous water-quality monitoring.

Figure 10-3. *Data buoy designed for monitoring water-quality parameters*

Figure 10-3 Prototype developed for monitoring Aqua ponds. A KiCad-based simple circuit board is designed for a water buoy. It includes an ADS1115 module for collecting analog signals, an SD card reader for data acquisition, and an OLED display for monitoring purposes. The OLED, SD card reader, and RTC are connected via I²C communication. The analog water-quality sensors are connected to the ADS1115 module. A DS18B20 digital temperature sensor is connected via digital GPIO pins to a 4.7K ohm transistor. Figure 10-4 provides the KiCad design for the data buoy.

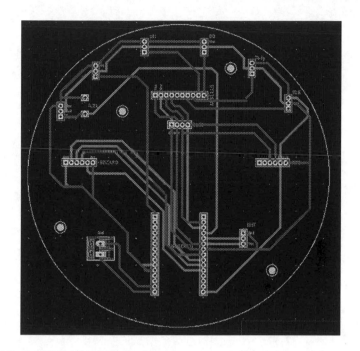

Figure 10-4. *KiCad PCB design*

A KiCad 3D view of the designed PCB board is shown in Figure 10-5.

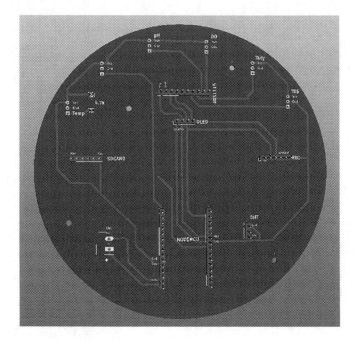

Figure 10-5. *Kicad 3D view*

The sensor discussed in the previous chapter is mounted with a
3D-printed housing module. The waterproof 3D printed module provides
water isolation between the electronics and the sensors. Figure 10-6
showcases the 3D design and the printed mounting module.

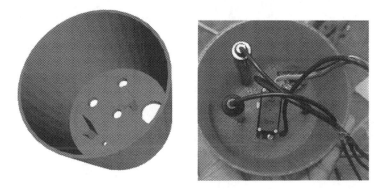

Figure 10-6. *3D printed sensor housing module*

The following is the firmware code.

```
//nodemcu code
#include <Arduino.h>
#include <ESP8266WiFi.h>
#include "HTTPSRedirect.h"
#define SensorPin A0
#include "DHT.h"
#define DHTPIN D4
#define DHTTYPE DHT11
DHT dht(DHTPIN, DHTTYPE);
#include <SPI.h>
#include <Wire.h>
#include <Adafruit_GFX.h>
#include <Adafruit_SSD1306.h>
Adafruit_SSD1306 display = Adafruit_SSD1306(128, 32, &Wire);
#include <OneWire.h>
#include <DallasTemperature.h>
#define ONE_WIRE_BUS D3
OneWire oneWire(ONE_WIRE_BUS);
DallasTemperature sensors(&oneWire);
float Celcius=0;
unsigned long int avgValue;
float b;
int buf[10],temp;
#include <Wire.h>
#include <Adafruit_ADS1X15.h>
const char* ssid     = "IoT";
const char* password = "IoT@1234";
//const char* ssid     = "Akash";
//const char* password = "Akash@1234";
Adafruit_ADS1015 ads1115;
```

```
// Enter Google Script Deployment ID:
const char *GScriptId =
"********************************bGnLR5aoXjCBJgehgkIlrA";
// Enter command (insert_row or append_row) and your Google
Sheets sheet name (default is Sheet1):
String payload_base =  "{\"command\": \"insert_row\", \"sheet_
name\": \"Data\", \"values\": ";
String payload = "";

// Google Sheets setup (do not edit)
const char* host = "script.google.com";
const int httpsPort = 443;
const char* fingerprint = "";
String url = String("/macros/s/") + GScriptId + "/exec";
HTTPSRedirect* client = nullptr;

// Declare variables that will be published to Google Sheets
float value0 = 0;
float value1 = 0;
float value2 = 0;
float value3 = 0;
float value4 = 0;
float value5 = 0;
float value6 = 0;
void setup() {

  Serial.begin(9600);
  delay(10);
  Serial.println('\n');
  ads1115.begin();
  sensors.begin();
  dht.begin();
  display.begin(SSD1306_SWITCHCAPVCC, 0x3C);
```

```
display.display();
delay(1000);
display.clearDisplay();
display.display();
display.setTextSize(0.5);
display.setTextColor(SSD1306_WHITE);
display.setCursor(0,0);
display.print("DBT Brackish Water");
display.display();
// Connect to WiFi
WiFi.begin(ssid, password);
Serial.print("Connecting to ");
Serial.print(ssid); Serial.println(" ...");

while (WiFi.status() != WL_CONNECTED) {
  delay(1000);
  Serial.print(".");
}
Serial.println('\n');
Serial.println("Connection established!");
Serial.print("IP address:\t");
Serial.println(WiFi.localIP());

// Use HTTPSRedirect class to create a new TLS connection
client = new HTTPSRedirect(httpsPort);
client->setInsecure();
client->setPrintResponseBody(true);
client->setContentTypeHeader("application/json");

Serial.print("Connecting to ");
Serial.println(host);

// Try to connect for a maximum of 5 times
bool flag = false;
```

```
  for (int i=0; i<5; i++){
    int retval = client->connect(host, httpsPort);
    if (retval == 1){
        flag = true;
        Serial.println("Connected");
        break;
    }
    else
      Serial.println("Connection failed. Retrying...");
  }
  if (!flag){
    Serial.print("Could not connect to server: ");
    Serial.println(host);
    return;
  }
  delete client;    // delete HTTPSRedirect object
  client = nullptr; // delete HTTPSRedirect object
}

void loop() {
int16_t adc1, adc2, adc3;
  adc1 = ads1115.readADC_SingleEnded(1);
  adc2 = ads1115.readADC_SingleEnded(2);
  adc3 = ads1115.readADC_SingleEnded(3);
  for(int i=0;i<10;i++)       //Get 10 sample value from the
                              sensor for smooth the value
  {
    buf[i]=analogRead(SensorPin);
    delay(10);
  }
  for(int i=0;i<9;i++)        //sort the analog from small
                              to large
```

```
{
  for(int j=i+1;j<10;j++)
  {
    if(buf[i]>buf[j])
    {
      temp=buf[i];
      buf[i]=huf[j];
      buf[j]=temp;
    }
  }
}
avgValue=0;
for(int i=2;i<8;i++)                       //take the average
                                           value of 6
                                           center sample

  avgValue+=buf[i];
float phValue=(float)avgValue*5.0/1024/6;  //convert the
                                           analog into
                                           millivolt
phValue=3.5*phValue;                       //convert the
                                           millivolt into
                                           pH value

Serial.print("     pH:");
Serial.print(phValue,2);
Serial.println(" ");
Serial.print("AIN1: "); Serial.println(adc1);
delay(300);

sensors.requestTemperatures();
Celcius=sensors.getTempCByIndex(0);
float h = dht.readHumidity();
float t = dht.readTemperature();
```

```
// create some fake data to publish
value0 = phValue;
value1 = adc1;
value2 = adc2;
value3 = adc3;
value4 = h;
value5 = t;
value6 = Celcius;

display.display();
display.println(value0);
display.println(value1);
display.println(value2);
display.println(value3);
display.println(value4);
display.println(value5);
display.println(value6);
display.display();

static bool flag = false;
if (!flag){
    client = new HTTPSRedirect(httpsPort);
    client->setInsecure();
    flag = true;
    client->setPrintResponseBody(true);
    client->setContentTypeHeader("application/json");
  }
  if (client != nullptr){
    if (!client->connected()){
      client->connect(host, httpsPort);
    }
  }
```

```
else{
  Serial.println("Error creating client object!");
}

// Create json object string to send to Google Sheets
payload = payload_base + "\"" + value0 + "," + value1 + ","
+ value2 + "," + value3 + "," + value4 + "," + value5 + "," +
value6  + "\"}";

// Publish data to Google Sheets
Serial.println("Publishing data...");
Serial.println(payload);
if(client->POST(url, host, payload)){
  // do stuff here if publish was successful
}
else{
  // do stuff here if publish was not successful
  Serial.println("Error while connecting");
}

// a delay of several seconds is required before
publishing again
delay(5000);
}
```

Figure 10-7 shows that the sensor data is collected in a corresponding Google Sheets programmed in NodeMCU. The data is updated every 10 seconds.

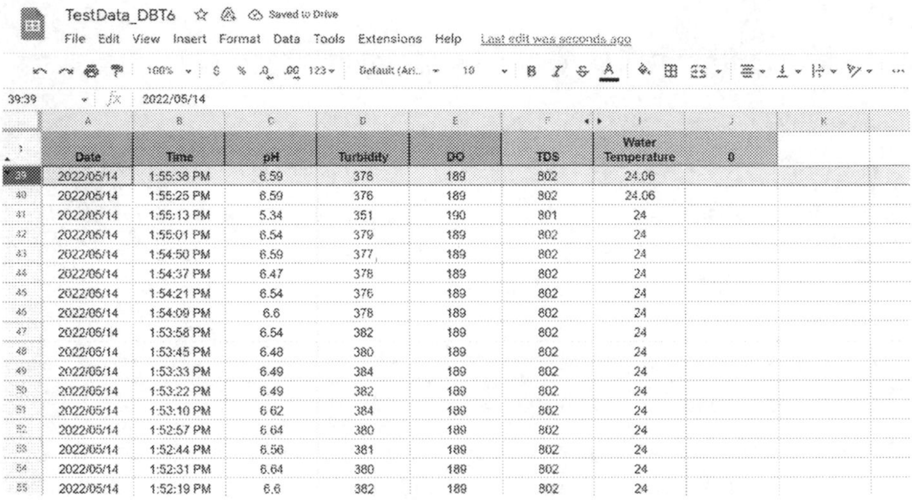

TestData_DBT6 Saved to Drive

File Edit View Insert Format Data Tools Extensions Help Last edit was seconds ago

39:39 fx 2022/05/14

	Date	Time	pH	Turbidity	DO	TDS	Water Temperature	0
39	2022/05/14	1:55:38 PM	6.59	376	189	802	24.06	
40	2022/05/14	1:55:25 PM	6.59	376	189	802	24.06	
41	2022/05/14	1:55:13 PM	5.34	351	190	801	24	
42	2022/05/14	1:55:01 PM	6.54	379	189	802	24	
43	2022/05/14	1:54:50 PM	6.59	377	189	802	24	
44	2022/05/14	1:54:37 PM	6.47	378	189	802	24	
45	2022/05/14	1:54:21 PM	6.54	376	189	802	24	
46	2022/05/14	1:54:09 PM	6.6	378	189	802	24	
47	2022/05/14	1:53:58 PM	6.54	382	189	802	24	
48	2022/05/14	1:53:45 PM	6.48	380	189	802	24	
49	2022/05/14	1:53:33 PM	6.49	384	189	802	24	
50	2022/05/14	1:53:22 PM	6.49	382	189	802	24	
51	2022/05/14	1:53:10 PM	6.62	384	189	802	24	
52	2022/05/14	1:52:57 PM	6.64	380	189	802	24	
53	2022/05/14	1:52:44 PM	6.56	381	189	802	24	
54	2022/05/14	1:52:31 PM	6.64	380	189	802	24	
55	2022/05/14	1:52:19 PM	6.6	382	189	802	24	

Figure 10-7. *Google Sheets screenshot*

References

[1] Mahesh Salunke, Amol Kalyankar, Chandraprakash D. Khedkar, Mahesh Shingare, and Gulab D. Khedkar, "A Review on Shrimp Aquaculture in India: Historical Perspective, Constraints, Status and Future Implications for Impacts on Aquatic Ecosystem and Biodiversity," *Reviews in Fisheries Science & Aquaculture,* vol. 28:3, pp. 283–302. doi: 10.1080/23308249.2020.1723058.

[2] Anjani Kumar, Pratap Birthal, and A. Badruddin, "Technical Efficiency in Shrimp Farming in India: Estimation and Implications," *Indian Journal of Agricultural Economics,* vol. 59, Jul–Sep 2004, pp. 413–420.

[3] Ravi Patel and Bhanu Sharma, "Shrimp farming," June 2022.

[4] Shiv Malvi, "A Study on Shrimp Farming and Surveillance," IJRASET, 2022.

[5] João Guimarães, "Shrimp Culture and Market Incorporation: A Study of Shrimp Culture in Paddy Fields in Southwest Bangladesh," *Development and Change*, vol. 20, October 2008, pp. 653–682. doi: 10.1111/j.1467-7660.1989.tb00361.x.

[6] Gurkan Tuna, Orhan Arkoc, and Kayhan Gulez, "Continuous Monitoring of Water Quality Using Portable and Low-Cost Approaches," *International Journal of Distributed Sensor Networks*, June 2013. doi: 10.1155/2013/249598.

[7] Yogendra Singh Parihar, "Internet of Things and Nodemcu A review of use of Nodemcu ESP8266 in IoT products," *JETIR*, vol. 6, June 2019, pp. 1085.

Index

A

Aerosol particle sensors, 51
Animation function
  classes, 155
  live line graph, 155–157
  oscilloscopes live, 157, 159, 160
Application-level network
    protocols, 96
Application programming interface
    (API), 173
Arduino programming, 76
  GSM/GPS modules, 177–180
  serial communication, 176
Autocorrelation graph, 133, 134
Automobile systems, 22, 23
axes.cohere() function, 131
Axes.twinx method, 136
Axes.xcorr() function, 132

B

Bar graphs
  categorical data, 118
  grouped bar, 118, 119
  horizontal bar, 122, 123
  proportional, 117
  stacked bar, 120, 121

Blemish sensors, 33
Bluetooth, 8, 175–177
Broadcasting data, 193, 194

C

Camera serial interface (CSI), 85
Carbon monoxide (MQ7), 58
Cartesian coordinates, 124
Central Institute of Brackishwater
    Aquaculture (CIBA), 266
Coherence, 131
Communication protocols, 8, 10,
    11, 28, 69, 75, 76, 227, 228
Contact sensors, 67–68
Coriolis flow meter, 63
Cross-correlation graph, 132, 133

D

Data lists, 137
Detectors, 31, 32, 36, 42, 43, 48, 50,
    54–57, 60, 66, 68
Dimension, 16, 59, 65, 148
Donut chart, 142–144
Dust sensor, 52
Dynamic Host Configuration
    Protocol (DHCP), 190